THE

NATIVE LITERATURE OF BOHEMIA

IN THE FOURTEENTH CENTURY.

FOUR LECTURES DELIVERED BEFORE THE UNIVERSITY

OF OXFORD ON THE ILCHESTER

FOUNDATION.

BY A. H. WRATISLAW, M.A.

HEAD MASTER OF THE GRAMMAR SCHOOL, BURY ST. EDMUND'S, AND FORMERLY
FELLOW AND TUTOR OF CHRIST'S COLLEGE, CAMBRIDGE.

LONDON:

GEORGE BELL AND SONS,

YORK STREET, COVENT GARDEN.

1878.

CHISWICK PRESS:—CHARLES WHITTINGHAM, TOOKS COURT,
CHANCERY LANE.

PREFACE.

HE interest expressed in the subject of the following Lectures (which were delivered in the Taylorian Institution in April and May, 1877, according to the terms of Lord Ilchester's bequest) by several of the audience, and the absolute absence of information upon it in the English language, have induced me to lay them before the British public. May I hope that the countrymen of Wickliffe will welcome an account, with specimens, of the Bohemian literature of the century which formed the dauntless hero and martyr of the next, Magister John Huss?

A. H. Wratislaw.

School Hall, Bury St. Edmund's,
    Dec. 10th, 1877.

CONTENTS.

LECTURE I.

NTRODUCTORY Remarks—State of Education in Bohemia in the 14th century—Queen's Court Manuscript — Discovery in the Library of Trinity College, Cambridge—Dalimil's rhymed "Chronyka Czeská"—Specimens—Legend of St. Catherine—Specimens —Alexandreis —Specimens —Chivalrous Literature—Hymns—Contest between the Soul and the Body—" Truth "—Legend of St. Procop—Specimen

pp. 1—42

LECTURE II.

Satirical Poetry—Satire " On Wicked Smiths "—Poem on the Ten Commandments—Bigamy—Adaptation of an Indian Tale—The Confessional—The " Anticlaudianus "—Specimen —Lord Smil Flaska—The New Council of Animals—Speci-

mens—"Wise Counsel of a Father to a Son"—Specimen—
"Contest of Water and Wine"—Specimen—"The Groom
and the Scholar"—Specimen—Poem on the Death of the
Blind King of Bohemia at the Battle of Creçy.   . pp. 43—76

LECTURE III.

Rise of Bohemian Prose—"Book of the Old Lord of Rosenberg"
—Specimens—Legends of St. Cyril, St. Methodius, and St.
Ludmilla of Bohemia—Translations of the Scriptures—Life
of Christ—Specimen—Albertus Magnus's "Book of the Vir-
tues" — Specimen — Pulkava's "Chronicle" — Specimen —
"Autobiography of the Emperor Charles IV."—Specimen—
Coronation Service— Specimen — "Ordo Judicii Terræ"—
Specimens — Andrew of Dubá's "Exposition of the Common
Law of the Land of Bohemia"—Specimens—Tkadleczek—
Specimens   .   .   .   . pp. 77—121

LECTURE IV.

THOMAS OF STITNÝ, Theologian, Homilist, and Philosopher—
Conclusion .   .   .   . pp. 122—165

THE NATIVE LITERATURE OF BOHEMIA
IN THE FOURTEENTH CENTURY.

I.

SCENE laid on the sea coast of Bohemia proves that Shakespeare had no very exact knowledge of the geographical position of that country, although it had given a queen, the good Queen Anne, to his own nation. And at the present time the people of Great Britain are for the most part in a similar state of ignorance with regard to the literature of Bohemia, scarcely believing indeed that it has any literature at all, and utterly unable to account for that great intellectual and religious revolution, which, in the beginning of the fifteenth century, shook the power of Rome to its foundations, and animated a Slavonic people of only four millions to maintain successfully a single-handed conflict against the Papacy and the German Empire for full two hundred years. And if it yielded at length to overwhelming numbers and weight, it was not until it had been undermined for nearly a century by the crafty and cruel policy of scions of the Hapsburg dynasty upon its throne.

It is a very unfortunate circumstance that so much of Bohemian literature has been lost, or rather ruthlessly destroyed by the emissaries and agents of the Church of Rome. So that we are really ignorant whether comparatively good or average or inferior works, especially in poetry, have reached our times; the selection not having been made by the deliberate judgment of posterity, but by the mere fact of escape from the fangs of Jesuit and other " missionaries," whose exact period is given by Dr. Palacky as ranging from 1620 to 1760, and afterwards from the more sporadic ravages of later destroyers. It mattered little to such barbarians whether any work that fell into their clutches was of Catholic or Protestant tendency, if it were but in the detested Bohemian tongue; and one Jesuit boasted on his death-bed that he had destroyed with his own hands no less than 60,000 volumes in that language.

Education reached a high pitch in Bohemia in the fourteenth century, and it is simply due to hostile calumny and its ignorant reception that the Bohemians in general and the Hussites in particular are commonly represented as a set of rude and ferocious barbarians, little, if at all, better than the Huns of Attila. The University of Prague itself was not founded till 1348, but efforts had previously been made in the same direction; and we are assured by Dr. Palacky ("History of Bohemia," vol. iii. pt. i. pp. 185, 186), that before the end of the fourteenth century every market town had its grammar school, and at least one-third of the country parishes their respective parish schools, and this over and above the schools attached to various monasteries and convents. Indeed such a state of general education was an absolutely necessary condition of such a movement as that inaugurated by Huss and his precursors, and carried on by a succession of statesmen and warriors with an ability and power which has only to be known to be appreciated, but which in this country is very little known and consequently very little appreciated.

I am not about to discuss the question of the genuineness of the Queen's Court Manuscript, which is commonly ascribed to the *thirteenth*, whereas I am confining myself to the undoubted remains of the literature of the *fourteenth* century. I will only remark, that every argument that has been brought against it, save one, admits of easy and victorious refutation. And that one is the absolute excellence of the unrhymed poems contained in it, which are decidedly superior to anything else in extant Bohemian poetical literature. Of one thing I am quite certain, namely, that the Queen's Court Manuscript was not forged either by the discoverer, Hanka, or by any one to whom he had access—to such an extent did he both misread and misunderstand it. But the fourteenth century is especially interesting as exhibiting the preparation for the great Hussite movement, and also as being the epoch of the rise of Bohemian prose, which only needs to be known to occupy a high place in the literature of the world.

I cannot forbear commencing with an account of

a discovery made in the Library of Trinity College, Cambridge, only two years ago. A manuscript had lain there unnoticed for 140 years, when the Rev. R. Sinker, the present librarian, observed it, and thought I might possibly be able to say in what language it was written. He asked me to examine it, and I recognized it at once as what is commonly called " Dalimil's Chronika Czeská," a rhymed chronicle of the second decade of the fourteenth century, tracing the Bohemians, or rather Czechs, from the Tower of Babel to the writer's own day. The author appears to have been a Bohemian knight, name unknown, who flourished between 1281 and 1314. The Cambridge Manuscript turns out to be the oldest complete (or nearly complete) manuscript of the work, and is ascribed to the year 1350 or thereabouts, only two fragments being of older date. I obtained the loan of the manuscript from Trinity College, and copied the whole, above 230 pages, for the Bohemian Museum. The writer gives his reasons for composing his work as follows—my translation being line for line with, and only varying from, the original by the substitution of an iambic for a trochaic rhythm of the same number of syllables :—

Many in histories delight,
Save that their own land they do slight;
Courtly therein their dead and wise,
Simple their own race in their eyes;
For had they look'd for honour there,
Books of their own land sure there were,
Whence they might know all their own race,
And whence they came might rightly trace.
I've sought such books for many a day,
And this hath been my wish alway,
That some one this to pass would bring—
Bohemia's deeds together string.
So long this end I wish'd to gain,
Till I the fact did ascertain,
That none therein would venture make—
Myself I will it undertake.
'Tis hard a chronicle to write,
From various sources to indite,
For what men say is all too true,
That nowhere is *the whole* in view.
The scribes did little zeal affect,
And therefore much they did neglect;
Each on his own small district thought,
Cared little for the rest or nought;
Did oft by brevity confuse,
And thus the sequence true did lose.
In Boleslaw a book I found,
Which above others did abound;
In wars it gave me special lore,
And taught me much unknown before.
Read'st thou of Prague the chronicle,

I do assure thee true and well,
Far fewer facts set down there are,
Though words are more abundant there ;
The Opatovian oft doth stray,
Deludes thee, though it more doth say ;
The Vyssegradian pleases least,
But that of Boleslaw is best.
Let all men, therefore, mark and know,
To this I hold, by this I go.
Find'st thou aught otherwise display'd,
Not by my will the change was made,
But as it written there we see,
So is it here set down by me.
Vain words t' abridge is my intent,
But give in full the sentiment,
That ev'ry man may learn from me,
And for his nation zealous be.
Hearing, the wise will wiser be,
The sad be set from sadness free.
I'll set things down as best I can,
And then entreat a better man,
Both for the honour of our land,
And craft of foemen to withstand,
My speech with rhyme to beautify,
And deck with graceful brilliancy ;
Nor words of jeering will he say :
E'en the unlearned chatter may.
In one thing I have conscience fair,
That I for my own tongue do care,
This has awoke the thought in me,
And urged me on to energy.

As a specimen of Dalimil's narrative style I give the death of St. Wenceslas, or, as the Bohemians call him, Vaceslaw or Vaclaw—c being pronounced as ts. He was murdered by his brother Boleslaw in A.D. 928.

His brother envy 'gan to pain,
He wish'd the crown and land to gain,
But only thus could show his spite:
Him to a feast he did invite,
Made for his son a christ'ning glad,
But evil in his mind he had.
While with his brother he did bide,
A godly squire who dwelt beside,
Brought him a saddled steed to ride:
"Mount and be off with speed," said he ;
"For evil here awaiteth thee.
Thy brother plans thy death, that he
In the whole land sole prince may be."
To whom the prince : "What thou dost tell,
Brother, I know myself full well.
All thank for thy fidelity,
But life's been long enough for me ;
If I for God can suffer nought,
Thus to my death will I be brought:
In honour of St. Michael I will drink this cup,
That he my soul may bear unto heav'n's kingdom up."
It was that cup in mind he bore,
Whereof God's Son did say of yore :
"If ye can drink that cup of pain,
Which to the dregs I now must drain"—

When he began to bid farewell—
" Here ye no more will see me dwell."
    To church, to prayer he took his way,
There Boleslaw did for him stay.
When Vaclaw saw his brother there,
He thank'd him for the banquet fair.
Said Boleslaw his brother to,
As from the sheath his sword he drew :
" Brother, I'm glad to serve thy will,
And now will likewise serve thee still ;
An end shall to thy speeches be "—
Down on his head his sword brought he ;
Yet was he ta'en with such affright,
The sword the skin could scarcely bite,
Yet off was smitten Vaclaw's ear ;
Down fell the murd'rous sword for fear.
The prince the sword doth raise and say :
" Brother, I might thee now repay ;
But so my God I love and dread,
Not for the world thy blood I'd shed."
This said, the sword he gives him back :
" Thy deed to finish be not slack : "
The church's threshold kneeleth on ;
Him Boleslaw doth rush upon,
Doth summon people to his aid,
While of him loud complaint he made.
Styrsa, Hnevisa with their brethren come,
And part the soul the body from.

An edition of Dalimil is now being prepared by
Dr. Josef Jireczek, which will give the text from the

Cambridge Manuscript, as far as it goes, evident gaps and mutilations being supplied from a manuscript lately discovered at Vienna of about twenty years later date. This edition would have appeared long ago, had not the discovery of the Cambridge Manuscript furnished the means of approaching far more closely to the original text than had ever been expected. It will also contain two ancient German translations of the Chronicle, so that it will be partially accessible to persons not acquainted with Bohemian.

In 1850 a manuscript of a long poetical Legend of St. Catherine was discovered by Dr. Josef Peczirka in the Royal Library at Stockholm, which uses words previously only found in the Queen's Court and Grünberg Manuscripts, approaches very closely in its language and style to the "Alexandreis," of which more anon, and is certainly a poem which would be considered graceful and elegant in any language. This legend places the martyrdom of St. Catherine on the 27th of December, whereas the Roman Church commemorates her on the 25th and the Greek on the 24th of November. The manuscript belonged to the Library of Peter Vok Ursinus of Rosenberg (ob. 1611), and was carried off by the Swedes in 1648, thus perhaps escaping destruction in its own country.

The extract of which I am about to give a translation requires a slight preface. Catherine, still a heathen, has received from a hermit a picture of the Virgin and child, which has wrought powerfully upon her imagination, and that the more as the face of the child is concealed from sight :—

> When people all were fast asleep,
> All fires gone out and darkness deep,
> It enters then into her mind,
> That her own bower she will find,
> That she a taper clear will light,
> And, taking out that picture bright,
> Will set it down before her there.
> Then with both hands she did not spare,
> But did her gentle bosom smite,
> While streaming from her eyes so bright
> Tears, bitter tears, run down her cheeks,
> As she to that fair virgin seeks,
> To save her from despair and be
> Pleased to allow her eyes to see
> The face of her belovèd son.
> With feelings sensitive o'erdone,
> With heart opprest, she sad doth sue,
> Saith, " Not as spouse, but handmaid true,
> Let him accept me, hapless maid ! "

Down her white cheeks, as this she said,
The tears did as a torrent stream ;
Bloodshot her eyes with anxious gleam,
Through longing great and earnestness.
When thus, in manifold distress,
Much had she wept in sore dismay,
Down sinking on the ground she lay,
And slept from utter misery.
    Then, then it was her hap t' espy
A vision full of high intent
And beauty and encouragement.
Her seemèd, as she slumber'd there,
She stood upon a meadow fair,
A meadow large, a meadow wide,
Full of delight on ev'ry side ;
With early summer grass 'twas bright,
So youthful blooming in her sight,
With ev'rything that's rich and fair,
As she lay slumb'ring dreaming there,
That as the things of this world go,
Pastures and meadows here below,
She'd never fairer, brighter seen,
Since she a living wight had been.
From these fair sights she turns her eyes,
And sitting on a throne espies
Mary, that gentle maiden bright,
Whose mother holy Anna hight ;
In arms she holds her only one,
The Christ, her own belovèd Son,
Embracing her with loving cheer ;
Above his little shoulder dear

His white neck glitters fair and bright,
E'en as a lily glitters white,
When fairest white its petals gleam;
And bright his lovely ringlets beam,
All pure and spotless to behold,
As beameth pure and precious gold,
Than other gold more precious still;
Upon his shoulders at their will
The curling ringlets waving roll'd,
In fashion like as rings of gold,
Of purpose made and with intent.
Sad sorrow to her heart was sent,
And in her thoughts was grievous woe;
For round and round though she did go,
Still of her wish was she beguiled—
To see the face of that fair child.

I will also give the scene on the way to martyrdom:—

They led her past the city's wall
And sadly gazed the people all,
That follow'd her upon her way;
And many a pagan lady gay
Was weeping there to be espied,
As she her lovely form descried,
And look'd upon her beauty bright,
Wailing the woeful time and sight,
That such a beauteous maiden fair,
So noble and of wisdom rare,
Must pass by shameful death away.
Then to her one and all cried they,

With flatt'ring words and blandishment,
And counselling with one intent,
That she herself therefrom should free,
And not allow unworthily
Her youth before its time t' expire,
But, as the Emp'ror did desire,
Should be a mighty Empress made,
And thus that grievous death evade.
Meanwhile their steps the plain have found,
And holy Cath'rine, looking round
Upon them, unto them doth cry :
" O all ye foolish people, why
Look ye on me in mournful guise,
And on me gaze with longing eyes ?
Ye men, and eke ye women, weep
For your own grief and take no keep
Of woes unreal, nor pity me,
Nor loudly wail my death to see,
Wherein small loss is mine to fear ;
But O ! if any standing near
Good will and kind compassion share,
Because my outward form is fair,
Me and my fate bewailing sore ;
These one and all I do implore,
To leave their wailing and their woe,
And in my glory joy to know,
All who stand sympathizing nigh.
And therefore this to you say I,
My heart this prayer doth urge, I ween,
For I with mine own eyes have seen
Christ Jesus' gracious self in sight,

Who is my very heart's delight,
Whose mighty power doth conquer all,
Who me unto himself doth call.
He is my energy and might,
He is my love and dear delight,
He is my King and Emp'ror great,
He my soul's aid in woeful state,
His is my bridegroom wise and dear,
He is my beauteous husband near,
Towards whom upsprings both mind and sense,
For he is perfect recompense,
In whom his saints full comfort know,
Elect in pure faith here below."

It is uncertain whether the translations of the " Alexandreis " current in Bohemia were made from the original poem in Latin hexameters, or from the German versions which were popular during the twelfth and thirteenth centuries. At any rate, the various fragments existing in Bohemian indicate that there were more versions than one current in the fourteenth century in the Bohemian language. As the original Latin is very scarce I give a couple of brief specimens, which will exhibit the style and sentiment of the poem :—

'Tis strange, O man, how thou dost toil,
And how thou dost thyself beguile,

> For pelf thy life adventuring,
> And e'en, a still more precious thing,
> Thy soul thou riskest day by day ;
> For pelf's dear sake with death dost play,
> Through water and through fire dost go,
> Not dreading aught of harm or woe,
> But always seeking pelf t' attain,
> Which yet thou must resign again,
> For brief and short thy little life.
> See, how this world in change is rife !
> To-day thou'rt sound and glad withal,
> To-morrow thou may'st breathless fall.
> Know, what from others thou dost gain,
> At death thou canst no more retain,
> Thou wilt not as the hills remain.

Alexander, encouraging his followers to enter upon the great campaign against Persia, relates a vision which had appeared to him shortly after his father's assassination :—

> But if a while ye will but wait,
> There's something that I would relate,
> Where-through I feel a certain hope,
> That with the foe we soon shall cope.
> 'Twas when my father dead was laid,
> A dream itself at night display'd :
> Methought, as there alone I lay,
> And none beside did watching stay,
> What counsel for myself to make ;

I knew not what to undertake,
Whether against my foes to rise,
Or lowly stand in slavish guise.
This did my mind distracted keep,
But all around were fast asleep.
I thought, as doth some wand'ring bird,
With confidence and trust deferr'd,
When she some quiet place doth seek,
Safely to keep her children weak,
Nor dares her nest with speed commence,
Lest sad misfortune drive her thence ;
The wind may chance the nest t' o'erthrow,
A snake may bring her young ones woe ;
Through field and woodland long she flies,
Till some choice place her eye descries.
E'en so it was my hap to gaze,
Till a clear light itself displays,
As from a storm-cloud lightning bright :
Whereat I was in dire affright,
Who, where I was no more I knew ;
Sudden from heaven's height in view
A man right beauteous to espy
Descended, and to me drew nigh.
All honour on himself he bore,
So wondrous was the garb he wore,
That verily my mind did ween,
That never man the like had seen.
Thus much for sure mine eyes did see,
A crown upon his head wore he,
That was of bright and burnish'd gold
And jewels precious to behold.

C

His name I could not learn at all,
And this alone to mind recall,
A name was on his forehead writ,
But I might not decipher it.
When I to him would question make,
First of himself his speech he spake :
" Go forth from thine own land," quoth he,
" All this world's fame I give to thee ;
If I hereafter meet thine eyes,
No evil think, no ill devise."
Thus briefly did he speak, and lo !
Whither he went no man doth know,
But as he turn'd himself away,
Vanish'd that light, nor more did stay ;
And thereupon my hope I build,
That what he said will be fulfill'd.

Of the chivalrous literature of the fourteenth century
I shall not give any specimens.   So far as yet published
it appears to be of British origin, and to consist of translations from the cycle of King Arthur and the Knights
of the Round Table.   The battle between Tristram and
Morolt is almost identical with the prose description of
the same combat in the " Morte d'Arthur," neither is
there any national or particular interest in the story of
Tandarias and Floribella.   Let me pass on to one or
two hymns and religious pieces, which are of consider-

able beauty and elevation of sentiment. The following hymn appears to have been written in a time of famine subsequently to the year 1378, when the great schism commenced in the Church of Rome.

> Our God Almighty rose
> From death, to save his foes :
> Then praise we him on earth,
> As Scripture bids, with mirth.
>   Kyrie Eleison.
>
> Three days he buried lay,
> He might no longer stay ;
> Pierced were his hands and feet
> For man's salvation sweet.
>   Kyrie Eleison.
>
> Jesus, thou didst arise,
> Ensample to our eyes,
> That we shall live again,
> And aye with God remain.
>   Kyrie Eleison.
>
> O Mary, Virgin dear,
> Bright rose from heaven's sphere,
> For us thy Son entreat,
> Whom as our Lord we greet.
>   Kyrie Eleison.
>
> Jesus, our Lord most dear,
> Thy realm and subjects hear,

Us sinful Christian men,
By all thou suffer'd'st then!
                    Kyrie Eleison.

O holy Mary's Son,
Forgive each sinful one,
Lord Jesus, in our need,
Thou who art ris'n indeed.
                    Kyrie Eleison.

O heav'nly King most dear,
Thy Czeskish people hear,
Relieve us from this dearth,
And plenty give on earth.
                    Kyrie Eleison.

In answer to our cry,
Peace and tranquillity
Grant, Jesu, glorious King,
That all thy praise may sing.
                    Kyrie Eleison.

Forgive our sinful state,
From error liberate,
And grant us bounteously
Thy Church's unity!
                    Kyrie Eleison.

O, all ye saints, entreat!
Aid us herein, as meet,
That we with you may dwell,
And Jesu's praises swell.
                    Kyrie Eleison.

The other hymn to which I shall invite attention possesses a peculiar historical interest of its own. It is alluded to by Huss himself in his sermon on Palm Sunday, where he says that the masters, priests, and scribes of his day cursed in the name of Jesus all those who went to Bethlehem (his chapel) to hear the sermon; all those who sang—

> God rose from death by his own might;

and, again, those who sang—

> O bounteous priest, Christ Jesu, Son,
> With Father and with Spirit one!

and, again, those who sang—

> Come, visit us, dear Christ, adored
> Of the whole world almighty Lord!
> Grant us in heart to know thee here,
> And to expect thee without fear!

The "Hymn to the Most Holy Sacrament" was discovered by W. Hanka on the back of a bond, dated 1398, in the binding of a book in the library of St. Vitus, at Prague, and runs as follows:—

> O bounteous Priest, Christ Jesu, Son,
> With Father and with Spirit one,
> Our all thy bounty is alone.
>   Kyrie Eleison.

Thou now before us dost appear ;
By all thy wounds and torments drear,
Have mercy, Maker, on us here.
              Kyrie Eleison.

Thy blood for us did freely stream,
From endless death did us redeem ;
Let bright forgiveness on us beam.
              Kyrie Eleison.

Angels, with chant and hymn, before
Their Maker kneeling low, adore,
And give him praise for evermore.
              Kyrie Eleison.

God's Mother, holy Mary dear !
Be thou well pleased to aid us here,
Grant us thy Son to know and fear.
              Kyrie Eleison.

Unto the Lord now let us cry,
Our guilt to pardon graciously,
And grant us heritage on high.
              Kyrie Eleison.

His Will alone our life doth give,
Then let us deeds of darkness leave,
And him no more to anger grieve.
              Kyrie Eleison.

O Father, Son, and Holy Ghost,
Count not our souls among the lost,
Complete the tenth choir of thy host.[1]
              Kyrie Eleison.

[1] Alluding to the mediæval interpretation of the parable of the

Of soul, of body Saviour free,
From deeds of ill our Guardian be,
And grant the soul thyself to see.
                    Kyrie Eleison.

O Holy Mary, aid our woe !
Ye Saints, your people help below,
Ere their souls perish evermoe !
                    Kyrie Eleison.

O Maker, feel not wrath severe
For sorrows of thy Mother dear,
For all thy pain and tortures here.
                    Kyrie Eleison.

We know that thou wast wounded sore,
Hands, feet, and side their anguish bore,
The scourge thy holy body tore.
                    Kyrie Eleison.

Thy blood and body, of thy grace,
As tokens of thy sacred face,
Thou here hast left us in thy place.
                    Kyrie Eleison.

By all thy pain and anguish sore,
By the five woes thy Mother bore,
For grief give joys for evermore.
                    Kyrie Eleison.

lost piece of silver. The nine pieces represented the nine orders
of angels ; the tenth and lost piece, the human race.

God is before us ; let us go,
And be his friends on earth below,
That he from heav'n may mercy show.
                    Kyrie Eleison.

Before us, holy Mary, go,
Entreat thy Son for us below,
For sinful Christians here in woe.
                    Kyrie Eleison.

Who chant this hymn in lowly state,
And on God's tortures meditate,
And duly them commemorate,
                    Kyrie Eleison

Let all a blessing here to-day
Receive, our sins to drive away,
Our sinful souls to save for aye.
                    Kyrie Eleison.

Seek we that fount unclosed for men,
That endless flames may spare us then ;
Answer we, one and all, Amen !
                    Amen, amen, amen !

The allegorical poem—the contest or dispute between the soul and body—demands rather a description than a specimen, especially as it is corrupt and defective in several places. The body is addicted to pleasure ; the soul sets its mortal nature before it, and complains that it will have to be punished for its sins.

The body dies, and the devil seizes upon the soul, which entreats the Mother of God for aid. Mary rescues the soul from the devil, and intercedes with her son for it, and he assigns it over to his judges— Truth, Peace, Righteousness, and Mercy—for judgment. The devil complains of injustice, but Mary defends the soul, and the judges also take its part. Peace promises to obtain grace for it from Jesus. The part of Mercy appears to be lost, as well as the conclusion of the poem. But the poem entitled " Truth " is both meritorious and entire, and I have translated the whole of it. It is found, with several other poems, in a manuscript written in the year 1426, at the Castle of Hasenstein. The metre is complicated, the stanzas running in pairs, and the last line of every even stanza rhyming with that of its predecessor, thus evidently exhibiting considerable practice in poetical composition.

PRAVDA (Truth).

In musings strange full oft I stray,
My heart to anguish sore a prey,
Thinking on life's unsteadfast way ;
To each and all,
How things befall,
The selfsame tale 'tis mine to tell.

Hear it, young son of honour'd age !
Hear it, thou old and hoary sage !
Deeds of th' unsteadfast world my page,
Alas ! must fill ;
This tale of ill
Full many know, few heed it well.

The world doth still God's anger earn,
The young the ways of virtue spurn,
The old with hate and discord burn,
For without shame
To paths of blame
The whole community doth tend.

TRUTH hath her dowry due no more,
Light is her value, as her store,
Crafty the change that Falsehood bore
Into her stead,
Where now as head
She rules, and Faith astray doth wend.

Alas, poor wretches, turn'd aside !
Your Truth is but a wand'ring wide,
And Falsehood judges you in pride
Of place.   Who gives,
Victorious strives,
Guilty is he whose gift is naught.

Thus Truth must suffer sorrow great,
Worse, ever worse, is her estate ;
The dawn arises dark as fate

With mists that fall;
'Tis doubtful all,
If sunshine e'er will back be brought.

Men heeded not, in haste t' acquire,
That silver, gold, their heart's desire,
Would some day loathsome be as mire—
Do sinners know,
Why thus they go,
Piling up wealth with toil and pain ?

Without a thought those lived their day,
Who honour own'd and wealth, that they
Like fools must die, and pass away
All nakedly
In poverty,
Knowing that we their place must gain.

Hear this, thou layer up of store !
Bethink thyself, I thee implore,
Thy bed must be beside the poor,
Where thou thyself
For all thy pelf
Betak'st, for death before thee lies.

Do worldly pleasures lead aside ?
A gloomy cavern yawneth wide,
Where thou for ages must abide;
There the great day,
That brings dismay,
Thou must await in poorest guise.

When stands that banquet[1] thee before,
Little the worth of all thy store,
Superfluous it for evermore.
'Tis then that friends
For selfish ends
Let envy step between and hate.

Thy pelf thy friends doth disunite,
Worms in thy body take delight,
Sin hath thy spirit in its might;
Each act and deed,
Each thought of greed,
'Gainst thy poor soul it doth relate.

The godly man is sore afraid,
Whom times of error have dismay'd,
For Truth they have commingled made
With Falsehood still
At their foul will,
As wore the world another dress.

All shame and fear are vanish'd quite,
Virtue and order put to flight,
Wherewith the world was sown aright:
Well blush may he
Who clear doth see
That wickedness doth Truth oppress.

From pope to king it is the same,
Both high and low all merit blame;

[1] Alluding to the funeral feast.

Truth is of little weight and name.
The priest before,
Without a store
Of gold, expect compassion small.

Not his to scorn a gift to take,
Doubt, anger, falsehood, to awake,
Both soul and body poor to make:
Who gold hath lost,
No less pays cost,
Or else no place to him doth fall.

Death only metes like measure aye,
Gives each man credit without pay,
Be he in scarlet clad or grey:
It promiseth,
Nor altereth,
But lodging gives to all aright.

There craft and craft's device are naught,
Nor aid of friends can profit aught,
So firmly are the limits wrought
For rich and poor
By edict sure
To come to judgment in the light.

Ah! that we feel so little fear
That death we have so sure and near,
As doth to each in turn appear;
When death draws nigh
Each heaves a sigh,
And needs unto his place must go.

Then gold and silver, heart's desire,
Loathsome to each appear as mire.
Poor wretches! In our danger dire
This thought be nigh,
In sin to die
Unto the soul is endless woe.

Fragments of sacred and comic plays are also extant, for instance, the " Quacksalver " and the " Divine Sepulchre," as well as legends in verse, of which specimens are given in Erben's " Vybor z Literatury Czeské." But the best qualities of all of these will be found in the legend of St. Procop of Bohemia, who flourished at the commencement of the eleventh century. It is contained in a manuscript of the early part of the fourteenth century discovered at König-grätz, and now in the Lobkovitz Library at Prague. This manuscript also contains seven satires on various trades and professions, a stupid fable about the Fox and the Pitcher, and a half didactic, half satirical poem on the Ten Commandments. The satires on the trades were printed for the first time in 1805, the other contents of the manuscript not till later.

The legend of St. Procop, scenes from which are to be found depicted or sculptured by the wayside in various parts of Bohemia, exhibits very strongly the resistance made to the introduction of the Roman ritual in place of the original Græco-Slavonic one. It is also in itself a curious legend; but, as might be expected in the case of a saint who interfered actively after death in opposition to the Church of Rome, it is not to be found in such works as Alban Butler's "Lives of the Saints." Although the manuscript itself is of the fourteenth century, corrupted rhymes and omitted lines indicate that the composition itself must be considerably older.

The writer commences by an address to old and young to listen to what he is about to tell them of St. Procop, "who was born in Bohemia, successfully extended his order, faithfully fulfilled the holy law, and wrought great miracles." The holy Procop, he continues, was of a Slavonic family in the village of Chotun, not far from Böhmisch Brod. His parents were an old farmer and his wife, who, according to Solomon's wish, were neither over rich nor over poor, but occupied in every respect a middle station. They were God-fearing people, and brought their son up in such a manner that he was soon remarkable for his

virtues amongst his equals. Seeing his excellence and
the bent of his mind, they sent him to Vyssegrad
(High-castle), near Prague, to a distinguished teacher,
under whom Slavonic learning and literature were flour-
ishing. Procop paid especial attention to the study
of the Scriptures, in which he made such progress that
all his teachers marvelled thereat, and remarked upon
it among themselves. He was never idle, and never
devoted any time to amusement; but was always engaged either in prayer or study, and was "as meek
and quiet as if he had been a monk." The canons
began to take notice of him, and, on account of his
humility, made him a priest and elected him a canon of
St. Peter's, and they would have elected him their
provost, had he not, in order to avoid the snares of
the world, refused to accept the position.

Meanwhile he met with a virtuous old Benedictine
monk, and requested him to admit him into his order.
The monk at first dissuaded him from giving up the
prospects before him in the Church of Bohemia, but
eventually consented to admit him. Procop then
adopted a hermit's life in the neighbourhood of his
native district, and finally settled in a forest near the

river Sazava, about ten English miles from Kourim. Here he found a rock, on which he proposed to dwell, preoccupied by devils. Undaunted by this, he proceeded to clear away the forest around, and built a chapel in honour of the Virgin Mary. For many years he remained here unknown to all men; but, as a city upon a hill cannot be hid, neither can a fire be under a bushel, so did not God allow him to remain unknown all his days.

A prince named Oldrich (Odalric, Ulric), after a discussion with his attendants as to where they should hunt, determined upon doing so in the hilly neighbourhood of the Sazava. In the course of the hunt the prince was left entirely alone, and a marvellously beautiful and well-fatted stag appeared before him. Oldrich pursued it, crossbow in hand, and it gradually retired before him, always just keeping out of range, till it reached the rock on which Procop was at work felling an oak. It sprang behind Procop, and turning its antlers towards him, displayed a cross between them.

> Seeing that beast of wondrous race
> And the monk so meek of face,

Prince Oldrich threw down his crossbow and pulled up

his horse.   He then proceeded to question the monk, asking him who he was and what he was doing there. The monk replied that he was a sinner named Procop, living in that hermitage under the rule of St. Benedict. Oldrich dismounted and begged him to hear his confession, which Procop did and assigned him a penance. After this the prince requested him to give him something to drink, as he was heated with his long chase. Procop replied that he had no other drink but the water which he drank himself.   Taking a drinking cup, he sighed from his heart, blessed the water with his hand, gave it to the prince, and bade him drink. On drinking, the prince was astonished at finding such excellent wine in so lonely a spot, and said that he had been in many lands, but had never drunk better wine.   Struck by these miracles, he bade Procop collect more brethren about him, for it was his intention to found and endow a convent there, which at Procop's recommendation he determined to dedicate to St. John the Baptist.   Oldrich took counsel with his lords and esquires, assembled workmen, and had the building erected with all possible speed, and Procop, against his will, was chosen abbot. This happened in the year of our Lord 1009, and in the reign of the Emperor Henry II.

Procop exercised all virtues and all hospitality, and various miracles of his are related at length. But just as the reverence for Procop was at its height, Prince Oldrich died without completing the convent as he had intended. His successor was his son Bretislaw, who being informed that Procop had been a hermit and then his father's confessor, and that his father had promised to build him a convent, but had died before he had fully carried out his intentions, proceeded to ask the advice of his councillors, who urged him to finish what his father had begun. He accordingly went to Procop, took him by the hand, commended himself to his prayers, addressed him as " Holy Father," and confirmed him in all possessions and privileges as abbot. Procop humbly besought him not to lay so great a burden upon him, but both the prince himself, Severus, Bishop of Moravia, and all present insisted on his holding the dignity and accepting the responsibility.

Procop was informed of his approaching death by Divine revelation two days before it happened. He communicated the intelligence to two of his friends, Vitos his sister's, and Jimram his brother's son, and also informed them that they would be driven from their convent by calumny, and compelled to seek refuge in a foreign land, where they would remain six years. He exhorted them to unity and love among themselves, and told them the names both of the prince who would persecute them, and of the one who would restore them to their convent.   His death took place, after two days' struggle with the devil, in the year of our Lord 1055, and his funeral ceremony was performed by Severus, Bishop of Prague. His gown was given to a leper whom he had himself previously desired to wait for it, and in a moment he was healed and his flesh became "as the flesh of a little child." The same person, who appears to have been also blind, desiring to see the body of Procop before it was put into the earth, was temporarily restored to sight for the purpose, but the cure was not permanent, as he was a professional beggar with a great disinclination for work.

After Procop's death the brethren took counsel together and elected the priest Vitos as their abbot. This man had been " the friend of his own soul, and was a person free from all wickedness, a wise man and full of grace." But in spite of all his excellence, misfortune came upon the brethren, which is thus related by the writer :—

> When Bretislaw, good prince, is gone,
> Ungracious Zbyhnew mounts the throne,
> Who little holds this convent dear,
> But lends to calumnies his ear.
> 'Twas thus the faithless work they plied,
> Thus to the prince they falsely cried:
> " O prince, there are Slavonians here,
> Another Scripture they revere,
> And divination practise still.
> Let them not, prince, thus work their will!
> In Slavic tongue the mass they sing,
> Before God's table clustering;
> Heretical their conduct bold,
> Such service in this land to hold."
> 'Gainst Vitos this and more they said,
> And those of whom he was the head.
> Their slanders had such force and strength,
> They drove them all away at length.
> Abbot and brethren, meeting there,
> Themselves to holy Procop's care
> Commended, then with hearts of woe
> Together did to Hung'ry go.
> To others then was given their place,
> To foreigners of German race.
> These Germans Latinists were known,

And glad that convent made their own.
O faithless trickery of hell!
O human envy, sad to tell!
O faithless sland'rers that ye be,
The devil's emissaries ye!
The devil whispers to you now,
Ere long hell-fires will round you glow.
Who doth God's servants harm and wrong
Will perish from the world ere long.
E'en thus those sland'rers it befell,
Who in this world not long did dwell.
Procop their deed right ill did take,
And to them on this wise he spake.
    They the first night to matins rose,
Each to the church in order goes,
There at the door did Procop stand,
And prophesied with upraised hand:
" Say, whence ye hither came to dwell?
What here hath been your business, tell!
Yea, who hath hither sent you, say?
Who this abode hath given you, pray?
What seek ye, sland'rers, here in sight?
What claim ye in this place of right? "
The Germans stood with fixed gaze,
But not a word a German says;
They all were awed in dire affright
At holy Procop's voice of might.
In terror great they speed away,
But yet thus much in answer say:
" Bohemia's prince, in order due,
His honourable council, too,

Us in this convent here did plant,
And it to us till death did grant."
When he a foreign language heard,
Procop continued thus his word :
"I warn you by God's power and grace,
Away, ye sland'rers, from this place !
If this ye shall neglect to do,
God's punishment will fall on you."
This said, he vanish'd from their sight ;
The Germans service held aright,
No heed unto his warnings gave,
But thought them trick'ry of a knave.

A second night was well-nigh spent,
The brethren to their matins went ;
The holy Procop came once more,
Stood in the church above the door,
Began to speak right angrily :
" Ye faithless Germans, tell me why
My warning thus with scorn ye treat ?
Here is for you no dwelling meet.
Yea, ye have done right faithlessly,
Hence chased my sons by calumny.
Hence, sland'rers, quickly from this place !
I give you warning now by grace."
Small heed thereto the Germans paid,
But turn'd to sport each word he said.
*   *   *   *   *
Till the third night he came in sight,
And did upon them show his might.
To them again he 'gan to say :
" Ye Germans hearken now, I pray,

I have fulfill'd God's Holy Writ,[1]
But ye my word regard no whit.
No place for you did I prepare,
For mine own sons I raised it fair ;
But, faithless sland'rers, not for you—
Ye are a vile Hungarian [2] crew !
The prince the convent gave, ye say,
But now I chase you hence away.
Good words could not your pride abate,
Sazava's home I'll make you hate.
Up ! on your road no moment waste ;
Take yourselves off to Prague with haste ! "
This said, his hand a cudgel bore,
With which he thrash'd the Germans sore.
No word the Germans dared reply,
But each man foremost strove to fly ;
No question ask'd they of the way,
But skipp'd along like goats at play.

They then went to the prince and told him to give the convent to whom he would: he would not get them to return thither, for they had been lucky to escape with their lives.

[1] By two warnings—one between them and himself, and one in the church. He could now treat them as heathen men and publicans. (Matt. xvii. 15—18.)

[2] Hungarian seems to have been a term of reproach in Bohemia, like "Dutchman" in England after the accession of William of Orange.

"That Procop," said they, "who lies there, will not allow us to possess his territories; and no one whom he does not favour can hold that convent. We have been in fear of him; let every man beware of such punishment."

The prince, hearing this, marvelled much, but did not think fit to repent and turn to God, "wherefore God shortened his days." Wratislaw succeeded him as Prince of Bohemia, sought out Vitos and the brethren, brought them back from Hungary, and replaced Vitos in his abbacy. "And thus was fulfilled the prophecy of the holy Procop."

However, Procop's saintly interference in support of the Slavonic ritual was only successful for a time. Discord broke out among the brethren, and in 1097 that ritual was entirely suppressed. But in 1348 the Emperor Charles IV. founded a Slavonic monastery in the new town of Prague, with a view to the eventual reconciliation of the Greek and Roman Churches. In this convent he placed monks from Dalmatia, Croatia, and other Slavonic countries, who made use of their own Slavonic ritual and the Glagolitic handwriting. Among other gifts, Charles presented the convent with

what was supposed to be the only relic of the old Bohemian Slavonic ritual still remaining, the Book of the
Gospels, part of which, in the Cyrillic character, was
said to have been written by St. Procop with his own
hand.   This Slavonic Codex, after various vicissitudes,
including a journey to Constantinople, obtained the
high honour of becoming the book upon which the
kings of France took their coronation oath at Rheims.

II.

ATIRICAL poetry has always been considered one of the most important aids to history, and that not so much from the mere facts that it records, as from the living picture that it enables us to lay before the mind's eye of scenes and modes of life which otherwise would have passed irretrievably into oblivion. It usually exhibits a correct, if sometimes one-sided view of society and social life in the day in which it is written, unless it be, what it rarely is, a mere slanderous libel on the times and contemporaries of the writer. The Bohemian satirical writings of the fourteenth century bear an impress of energy and reality upon them which makes them not only well calculated, but indispensable to assist us in forming an idea of the then social and intellectual condition of that remarkable people. And

although I cannot claim for them the wit and finish of
Chaucer's Prologue to his " Canterbury Tales," still
I think we shall be satisfied to assign them a fair
position in the literature of their century.   I proceed
to the consideration of the satirical poems contained
and preserved in the same manuscript which has given
us the legend of St. Procop.

The first satire, " On Shoemakers," is perhaps the
most amusing, but its character and colouring are
so local and so dependent upon little turns and touches
in the original, and upon various details which would
require long notes to illustrate them, that I have not
ventured to translate it, and instead thereof have
selected as a specimen the third, " On Wicked Smiths,"
which runs as follows :—

> Ye Smiths, mark well what now I say,
> From evil deeds refrain, I pray ;
> I warn you of a work of ill,
> That ye therefrom may keep you still.
> No sin, it seems, appears to you
> In that which many of you do ;
> Ye think it never is a sin
> Money in evil way to win.
> A thief doth on thy cottage light,
> Comes to thee in the stilly night,

Saith : " Hither, prithee, master dear !
A gift that's good I've for thee here,
If thou'lt in secret forge for me
That which I shall commission thee ;
If thou a mighty saw wilt make,
Wherewith I may all iron break,
That nought 'gainst it shall hold at all
Or be it great, or be it small ;
Whate'er of iron meets my view,
That saw shall cut it through and throug
Besides a knife of steel be mine,
That nought resists its keenness fine ;
Forge me a dozen keys likewise,
To which there's nought but open lies ;
All things, that in the world there be,
I at my will shall open free."

His orders given on this wise,
As to deceive he did devise,
Glad hears the smith what he hath said,
Comforts the thief with promised aid :
" All this I'll gladly for you do,
The knife, the saws, I'll make for you ;
But of my service mindful be,
And pay just recompense to me."

This said, the thief, to all awake,
Doth from his purse a guinea [1] take,
" This guinea " saith " I give to thee,
Another, when thou com'st to me.

---

[1] A *Verdunk* =16 Prague groschen. Germ. Vierdung=
¼ pound (our word farthing).

Deep in the forest us thou'lt find,
Leave not the saws, the knife, behind ;
There will I pay thee all aright,
Thy trouble and thy work requite."
    And thus the smith doth pelf acquire,
And glad with thieves consorts for hire.
    Another thing I know full well,
And ev'ry man thereof will tell ;
Whene'er a smith a horse doth shoe,
He freely makes this promise too :
" Thy horse I've shod right well," quoth he,
" A hundred miles he'll travel free :"
But scarce thou start'st from him to go,
The jade begins a limp to show.
I wish the Lord to me would grant
The thing that I just now do want ;
Would put a smith into my power—
He'd bedrid be from that same hour.
I'd wish a law to make below,
That smiths upon four feet must go :
The owner of an injured horse
The cruel nail should draw perforce,
And in the smith's foot stick it tight.
He'd cry to heaven with all his might,
He'd mind his shoeing without fail,
Nor to the quick poor horses nail.

The poem on the Ten Commandments commences in the most becoming and didactic manner, but ere long breaks out into extremely amusing satire. It is well known that in the Middle Ages a dead set was made by the celibate clergy against the second marriage of widows, and that widowhood was lauded and exalted as a state of life only second to virginity itself. If we turn to Shakespeare's " Richard III." (act iii. sc. 7), we find the Duke of Buckingham represented as endeavouring to brand the sons of Edward IV. with illegitimacy, not only on account of alleged precontracts with Lady Lucy and " Bona, sister to the King of France," but also by reason of his marriage with the *widow*, Elizabeth Woodville.

> These both put by, a poor petitioner,
> A care-crazed mother to a many sons,
> A beauty-waning and distressed *widow*,
> Even in the afternoon of her best days,
> Made prize and purchase of his wanton eye,
> Seduced the pitch and height of all his thoughts,
> To base declension and loathed *bigamy*.

Here Blackstone informs us that " Bigamy by a canon of the Council of Lyons, A.D. 1274 (adopted in England by a statute in 4 Edward I.), was made unlawful and infamous. It differed from *polygamy*, or having two wives at once; as it consisted in either marrying two virgins successively, or once marrying

a *widow*." Buckingham, in Shakespeare, represents
Elizabeth Woodville as entrapping Edward IV., but
the converse of the case is exhibited in the Bohemian
adaptation of an Indian tale, in which a pious widow is
depicted as made prize of by a lover, through the
agency of one of those godless beldams, who were only
too eager to seduce fair widows a second time into the
snares of matrimony, and thus into an alleged breach
of the Sixth (Seventh) Commandment.

> These and their tricks I know full well,
> And now thereof a tale will tell,
> How one, right cunning to mislead,
> As a good nun appear'd indeed,
> Did a fair widow guide astray,
> And made her tread the evil way.
> A wealthy youth with love was fired,
> And much this widow fair admired,
> And many a gift to her he sent,
> And fain his life with her had spent,
> But in his suit could prosper nought,
> Though wedlock honourably he sought,
> For she had vow'd, whate'er betide,
> A widow ever to abide.
> A time there came at length, when he,
> Sitting with her in converse free,
> Did ask her confidentially,
> Whether she'd be his wedded wife,

Or hear no more of him for life.
To him in answer then she said:
" Nor thee nor any man I'll wed ;
For I have ta'en a vow to be
Unto my death in purity."
The youth in sorrow fell that day,
And swoon'd well-nigh for grief away,
And from her presence sad did go
In misery and utter woe.
   When that old beldam saw his grief,
His sadness seeming past relief,
She sought with words to know his state,
Into his heart to penetrate.
Why was his spirit grieved and sad ?
What then had happ'd of ill and bad ?
He spurns her quick with anger free:
" Why busy thus, old hag, with me ?
What were the good, my pain and woe
Unto a slave like thee to show ?"
But ere his words an end had ta'en,
She answer gives to him again :
" Dear son, of this be sure as fate,
And to thy friends as true relate ;
As leech's skill can no man heal,
Save him who doth his wound reveal,
So none can cure thy grief of heart,
Dost thou to none its cause impart.'
The youth unto her straight replies
" I see thou art a woman wise,
And therefore, mother, I to thee
Will truly tell what vexeth me,

E

If thou wilt not my trust betray,
But out of sorrow find a way."
" Delay not, son, to tell the tale,
My help will, sure I am, avail."
" Mother, there is a widow here ;
I'd promise all my gold and gear,
If things to such a point were led
That I this widow fair might wed.
Long have I wish'd her hand to gain,
But nought have won by all my pain ;
And many a gift I've lavish'd free,
But woe and sorrow 'tis to me,
That she my suit doth scorn and slight,
And hath me now refused outright."
Saith she, " My son, revile me not,
But let a guerdon be my lot ;
Thou shalt not long in anguish wait,
But summon'd be unto her straight."
" O might this come to pass," he cried,
" A guerdon good should thee betide."
" Only be merry, son," said she,
" With her thou soon shalt happy be."
      Then 'gins that beldam old conceive
How she the widow can deceive,
Who was in honour'd purity,
And all her days the same would be.
She had a little dog, I ween,
Nice little dog as e'er was seen ;
This for three days she made to fast,
Till hunger pinch'd him sore at last ;
Then mix'd she mustard hot with bread,

And thereupon her doggie fed,
Then to the widow went with speed,
Doggie and all, to earn her meed.
   The lady deems her good and wise,
And welcomes her in friendly guise,
And when the twain together were,
They sate in various converse there.
Soon, when the dog the lady spies,
With tears fast streaming from his eyes,
" Tell me," saith she, " dear mother mine,
What ails this little dog of thine?
What causes thus his tears to flow,
Most like a human being's woe ? "
The beldam smote her bosom straight,
And 'gan to weep in woeful state.
" Dear daughter, heard'st thou ne'er," quoth
    she,
" How sorrow came to sinful me,
Sorrow that I dare not reveal,
But must for very shame conceal ?
When up you rise or down you lie,
Pray ne'er t' endure such misery,
Pray that thy friends nought such may know,
Nor wish such sorrow to a foe.
But, if thou'lt keep my secret still,
I'll tell thee, lady, all my ill."
" Dear mother, all in safety say,
Thy secret's safe with me for aye."
" I once possess'd a daughter dear,
Who now doth as a dog appear ;
This little dog, that here doth lie,

My daughter was in time gone by.
'Twas thus my sorrow sad did come :
When I was in my distant home,
I was a woman rich and high,
And in esteem none stood me nigh.
I had a daughter wondrous fair,
Of beauty and of prudence rare ;
She married, and her husband died,
And she a widow did abide.
Her beauty and her pelf in view
Full many a suitor to her drew ;
Amongst them one my daughter woo'd,
Whose kindred and whose friends were good ;
His love the rest far overwent,
And many a goodly gift he sent.
When thus were spent some years of life,
In hope he claim'd her for his wife,
But she, poor silly fool, was fain
An honour'd widow to remain ;
And answer giving to him, said :
' Nor thee nor any man I'll wed.'
But ah ! he loved her all too well,
And into melancholy fell,
Disease from melancholy spread,
And finally his spirit fled.
God's vengeance therefore on her came,
Her face and form a dog's became,
And she a dog must ever be,
Her punishment she may not flee.
The pious, daughter dear, take heed,
By others' fall and righteous meed ;

Hast thou of kin a lady near,
Hast thou a friend to thee right dear,
Who time in converse sweet has pass'd,
And scorn'd her lover at the last?
My daughter's hap thou know'st full well,
And canst to such another tell,
That she may 'scape like grievous end:
Each from such woe the Lord defend!"
" Dear mother, woe is me," said she;
" The self-same thing's been done by me.
What shall I do or say?" she cried.
" A youth had made me fain his bride,
A noble youth of noble race,
Goodness and wealth his kindred grace;
But I must still myself accuse,
His proffer'd hand I did refuse,
Although his love was deep and true,
And costly were his gifts nor few."
" I'm sorry for thee, daughter dear;
Herein thou hast done ill, I fear.
Look quickly into thine own heart—
True counsel this I do impart—
And thou wilt not transfigured be,
My daughter like, whom thou dost see."
" How can this be?" did she exclaim;
" I cannot to him speak for shame.
If thou my agent here wouldst be,
Wouldst talk to him again of me,
I'd give thee, as thou shalt require,
A guerdon to thy heart's desire."
The beldam said, " I know him not;"

But when her guerdon safe she'd got,
O then she went in shameless guise,
And claim'd the young man's gift likewise.
  Thus did this wicked beldam's wile
The youth and widow too beguile
Of gifts, and drew with crafty call
An honour'd widow to her fall.
A traitress such, we must confess,
Is worse than any murderess ;
Two souls, her own, a third, as well,
She murders by the might of hell.

It is singular that mediæval ecclesiastics should have borrowed their arguments against the re-marriage of widows from Sanscrit and heathen sources. The story first occurs in a Sanscrit book of the eleventh century ; but the widow there resists the temptress, while in the Christian adaptation she is beguiled. The machinery of the little dog is evidently derived from the doctrine of the transmigration of souls.

But, however erroneous we may consider the drift of this amusing apologue to be, the error is amply atoned for under the Seventh (Eighth) Commandment, under which the writer inveighs with righteous indignation against the grasping conduct of avaricious nobles, in

taking mean advantages of their " chlapi " or peasant
tenants. But the most interesting portion of the work
is that in which, under the same Commandment, he
runs on parallel lines with his contemporary, our own
Chaucer, in denouncing the corruptions of the regular
clergy, especially the begging friars, and that particularly in connection with the confessional. A man
comes to a friar, confessing himself guilty of all manner
of crimes. He has pillaged half a score of churches,
has robbed and murdered priests, has been a thief, an
incendiary, and a burglar; has never made restitution
to any one, and has wasted a large patrimony in evil
and riotous living. He asks for absolution and penance,
premising that he can neither fast nor go on a pil-
grimage, nor get up early in the morning; that he
doesn't like repeating paternosters, and is utterly
ignorant of any other prayer. The friar replies that
the matter is perfectly easy, if the penitent will but
hearken to his recommendations. The brotherhood to
which he belongs is very poor, and entirely dependent
upon such persons and their alms. He therefore proposes to absolve him from all his sins on receipt of a
single pound (hrivna), towards purchasing his friar's

habit.[1]   This causes the writer to burst out into an invective against wicked confessors, and to address confessors in general in the following strain:—

> Confessors! mark what now I say,
> And good example take, I pray!
> Of sinful souls yourselves ye call
> Physicians; this admit ye all.
> Know, each physician, faithfully
> Who'll help his patient's malady,
> Cures otherwise an ague chill
> And one with dysentery ill;
> Doth in one way the dropsy meet,
> And otherwise sore eyes doth treat;
> A diff'rent med'cine doth apply,
> If honest, to each malady.
> He would perchance cause greater woe
> Should he the selfsame salve bestow
> Upon inflamed or weakly eyes
> Which he unto a wound applies.

[1] Compare Chaucer's Prologue, 225 sqq.:—

> " For unto a poure ordre for to give
> Is signe that a man is wel i-schrive;
> For if he gaf, he dorste make avaunt,
> He wiste that a man was repentaunt.
> For many a man so hard is of his herte,
> He may not wepe although him sore smerte;
> Therfore instede of wepyng and preyeres,
> Men moot give silver to the poure freres."

So too, thou soul-physician, deal
In penance with like varied zeal :
Each manner sin, that men commit,
Craves corresponding penance fit :
The glutton bid to fast, and tell
Th' unchaste in purity to dwell ;
The thief bid restitution make,
From his own store with bounty take.
Each manner sin, that men commit,
Craves corresponding penance fit.
Mark what the scripture doth declare :
God from such sins absolveth ne'er,
Unless that is returned seen
Which hath unjustly taken been.
And this thyself remark thou well,
To all men this ensample tell,
That in good sooth no surgeon can
Handle and cure a wounded man,
Till knife or arrow, cause of pain,
Be from the wounded body ta'en.

    *   *   *   *   *   *

But glad were I, could it but be,
If I like recompense could see
For like confessors, one and all,
As did a chaplain once befall,
That did confess a robber strong
Who'd done to many force and wrong.
Quoth he, " Wouldst fain do penance well ?
A bargain good to thee I'll sell.
Whate'er thou'st stolen from thy youth
I free thee from all guilt in sooth ;

If gold from men thou'st ta'en away,
Give me a shilling here to-day."
" Sir priest, thy bidding soon were done,
But ready cash, alas! I've none.
On Monday to the wood repair ;
If God shall grant me fortune fair,
That shilling glad I'll give to thee,
And be from sin by penance free."
When comes the priest the wood unto,
He pays aright the shilling due,
And says : "A second too be thine,
And for it let thy horse be mine ;
Thy cassock too be mine this day,
And homeward wend on foot thy way.
For this one sin I've given more,
The truth to tell, than all before."

An unknown Bohemian poet has abridged rather than translated the "Anticlaudianus," a Latin poem in hexameter verse, of Alan of Ryssel (1114—1203), a priest of the Cistercian order at Clairvaux. Nature, deploring the moral corruption of the world, desires a perfect man to be created or begotten, and calls the Virtues to council. Wisdom or Prudence proposes that, as Nature can only produce what is material, she should apply to God with the petition to form such a man. Wisdom is sent to God with this petition in a chariot constructed of the Seven Sciences, with Reason as coachman, and drawn by the Five Senses. All that she sees in passing through the first eight heavens is described, and she is at length admitted into the ninth heaven, where God hears her prayer, and after consulting with his four daughters Mercy, Truth, Peace, and Faith, promises and effects the salvation of man by the incarnation of his Son. The manuscript containing this poem is in the library of the cathedral church of St. Vitus. I give as a specimen the description of the horses of the chariot:—

> The first horse is yclept the Sight,
> Who flows, as 'twere, with speedy flight
> O'er rock or wall or over seas,
> A thousand miles can run with ease,
> Nor ever wets his hoofs so fleet,
> Nor bends the grass beneath his feet;
> As flies a bird, he gallops ever,
> And on his way doth loiter never.
> This horse right meet the chariot finds,
> Unharm'd by work, no toil he minds,
> The second horse is Hearing named,
> For which this chariot is famed;
> This second horse is also fleet,
> And never doth he wet his feet;
> O'er seas, o'er water, goes, as ground,
> Well suited to the chariot found.
> The third horse is the Smell, I ween,

The fourth the Taste is harness'd seen;
The fifth horse is the Touch so light,
This noble chariot's dear delight.
All five indeed are horses fleet,
All five for this fair chariot meet.

We come now to Lord Smil of Pardubitz, surnamed
Flaska, one of the leading Bohemian nobles of his day.
The date of his birth is not known, but he is spoken of
as a full-grown man in documents of the year 1384,
and in 1395 he became a member of the union formed
by the Bohemian lords for the defence of the privileges
of their order against King Wenceslas IV. King
Sigismund was appointed umpire between his brother
Wenceslas and the insurgent nobles, and he, by his
decision, pronounced on April 2, 1396, assigned to
Smil Flaska the office of Chief Secretary of State in
the kingdom of Bohemia, an office which he held,
although not quite uninterruptedly, until his death.
From the side which he took in the politics of his day,
he came frequently into collision with the Bohemian
towns, and was killed in a skirmish with the citizens
of Kutná Hora (Guttenberg) between that place and
Czaslaw, on August 13, 1403. Besides a collection of
the most ancient Bohemian proverbs, he wrote the

"New Council" of animals in verse, and several other poetical works, which are certainly of his date, are also ascribed to him.

The "New Council" belongs to that cycle of didactic tales of animals which in the thirteenth and fourteenth centuries were current in France, in Flanders, in north-west Germany, and ere long in Bohemia also. Two other similar Councils of animals and birds of later date are extant in Bohemian. The manuscript in which Smil Flaska's "New Council" occurs is in the Bohemian Museum, and contains also, besides several prose works, "The Counsel of a Wise Father to his Son," and "The Contest of Water and Wine," both of which are ascribed to Smil Flaska. The plot of the "New Council" is this: After the death of old King Lion, the young King assembles together all his princes, nobles, and commons, both beasts and birds, and desires their advice for his future conduct. They advise him according to their several natures, some expressing noble and elevated sentiments, others urging him to tyranny and vice. I have selected the speeches of the Stag and the Camel, as exhibiting fair specimens of the style and sentiments of the writer.

THE STAG.

The Stag did next his counsel show,
And said : " Dear King, to war be slow ;
Whene'er thou canst, to peace incline,
For that most gracefully is thine.
Love thou not those whose deeds are ill,
Let justice with them reckon still,
With malefactors, faithless, dire—
Truth doth my vent'rous words inspire—
Let them not practise force and wrong,
But dwell thou still the good among,
Winning their love by fav'ring grace.
This say I now with honest face,
That all the world for this doth strive,
Longing at length in peace to live :
For thieves and robbers, warriors too,
For this end practise what they do,
Wishing by war such gain to make
That they in peace their ease may take.
For this their lawless deeds are done,
Yet thus their end is seldom won,
But peace from violence doth flee.
Therefore, O King, I say to thee,
Whoe'er by pride and restless mind
Peace for himself doth strive to find,
That man his peace not long will keep,
With him 'tis perilous to sleep.
For he whose gains ill-gotten be,
Not often is from danger free ;
When least expected, falls the blow

On him whose wealth from guilt doth flow.
Peace, peace is ev'ry one's intent,
Such has been aye my sentiment.
Full many know not how to dwell,
And peace they understand not well;
So precious 'tis, it has no price;
Once give up peace, by ill advice,
And peace henceforth your prayers will spurn,
And never to you back return.
Whoe'er an honour'd place attains,
A fool I call him for his pains,
If unconstrain'd he does it quit—
O King, I give thee counsel fit.
Thy ancestors in mem'ry bear,
Their rule how godly and how fair!
To God, to man, how dear were they!
Good mem'ries of them with us stay.
Their annals studying never tire,
And after actions good inquire,
That thou in the same steps mayst go,
And to the good all kindness show,
But to the bad severity,
That still the good unharm'd may be.
Thus thou wilt wealth and honour gain,
And seek God's mercy not in vain,
Which ev'ry faithful man doth prize.
Such things, O King, I thee advise."

THE CAMEL.

The Camel's figure was not fair,
His words though of the wisest were.

Quoth he: " Lay thou thereto thy heart,
Should sorrow cause a subject's smart;
Should widow sad or orphan poor
Oppression hard or harm endure ;
Should one with wrong assail them sore,
Take pity on them evermore.
If thou canst not avenge them straight,
Thy pity can upon them wait,
Can comfort and console their woe.
Who force and wrong doth undergo,
Fear not, but gladly to him go,
For better 'tis to seek a home,
Where's weeping, wailing, dreariment,
Than where is feast or merriment.
Wise words are wondrous in their kind,
And counter to the foolish mind,
To eye of owl as solar ray ;
Put thou, O King, such mind away,
Hear thou wise words with gladsome heart,
And after ponder them apart;
Let them within thy mem'ry dwell,
That thou mayst understand them well;
This to thy benefit will be,
Let shamefastness be aye with thee,
That thy true heart may ever fear
Whate'er licentious doth appear.
With pure thoughts have a mind well stored
Towards Jesus, thy beloved Lord ;
Have shame towards him and not towards men,
For ev'ry heart is in his ken,
Yea, not thy least light thought can be

Before thy God in secrecy.
Therefore I say, O King, to you,
In all thy deeds be pure and true,
In ev'ry place unceasingly;
Thus thou in the right path wilt be,
Which leadeth unto heaven's height,
And wilt be blest with dear delight.
Promise what in thy power doth lie,
Bind not thyself with promise high
Or work beyond what thou canst do;
Do all thou dost with measure due.
In actions and in words likewise
To keep the mean I thee advise.
Enough than much is better still;
Observe and mark this rule who will."

From the " Wise Counsel of a Father to a Son,"
which is also ascribed to Smil Flaska, I extract the following noble remarks on the effect of true and honourable love on a chivalrous young man :—

Who loves a maid with honour due,
Doth to her vow his service true,
Doth in that faith t' abide delight,
Good hope there is he'll be a knight
In deed and noble mind likewise.
Being with her in true love's ties,
Full of all honour for her name,
On foot, on horseback, all the same,
Towards God, towards man of feeling heart,
Bold for what hath in goodness part,

F

But timid towards whate'er is ill,
As a scared bird, that's frighten'd still.
For her sake evil doth he fear,
Her beauty is to him so dear ;
For her sake better is th' intent,
Wherewith his actions all are meant ;
So rich in hon'ring her is seen
His love, no touch of action mean
His very shadow can o'ertake,
Nor aught of sullen gloom can make
Disturbance in his cheerful mind,
Such strength that love, that faith doth find.
Therefore, my son, this maxim hold :
A maiden's love deem thou as gold,
Than precious stones more precious far,
That with it nothing can compare
Of all things in the world that are.

The " Contest of Water and Wine" is introduced in
a somewhat singular fashion. A " master of holy writ"
has eaten and drunk somewhat more than he ought
to have done, and is therefore left in a helpless condition by his convivial companions. In this position
he has a dream which he afterwards relates. He
dreams that he is carried up into the third heaven,
where he sees many wonderful things, and in particular is a witness to a contest between water and
wine, in which neither is at all sparing of the honour

or feelings of the other. Finally the master wakes up and induces them to elect him as umpire. They assent, and he cleverly makes use of the mixed chalice in the Eucharist to reconcile them.

> Both ceased to speak, and each th' affair
> Confided to the Master there,
> Who standing thus between the tway,
> Said : " Ladies mine, give ear, I pray!
> I now will tell you right and true
> That which I know is best for you.
> The Lord God, who created all,
> Did water form and wine withal,
> Water to laymen gave and wine
> Unto the clergy did assign.
> Both offspring are of God most high,
> Of princely grand nobility ;
> Could clergy without laymen stay ?
> What without clergy were the lay ?
> Neither estate can all supply,
> Nor praise, as due, the Lord on high.
> One without other cannot stand,
> As ev'ry man may understand ;
> Mass without wine there cannot be,
> Water to wine we added see,
> For God himself ordain'd it so—
> Who then is he that shall say No ?
> Who thus our faith destroy shall dare,
> A very Judas sure he were ! "

The satirical poem entitled " The Groom and the Scholar " (*Podkoní and Zák*) must not be passed over unnoticed. It is ascribed to Smil Flaska, but for no better reason than that it is found in the same manuscript as the " Wise Counsel of a Father to a Son." To my mind it is written in an easier and more flowing style than the " Wise Counsel," and it is certainly a good deal more witty than any other production of the reputed author. A groom and a scholar, or what we should now term a student, apparently in one of the minor orders, whose dress and appearance are elaborately described, meet in a public-house, salute each other and enter into conversation, at first politely enough. But ere long each begins to commend his own position and ridicule and vituperate that of the other. I give as a specimen one of the speeches of the scholar, which exhibits the social position of both parties pretty plainly. I must mention first that the scholar's liability to the rod has been particularly insisted upon by the groom, a liability which was shared by undergraduates at Cambridge at a comparatively late epoch—John Milton himself having received the last recorded birching in the buttery of Christ's College.

The scholar is one of those who, like his contemporary in Chaucer's prologue, had to beg for the " wherewith to scoleye."

> " Wishest thou still my company,
> I will from books relate to thee,
> What I of you did read one day.
> As one alone rode on his way,
> Seeking an honest servant lad,
> But ah ! no groom at all he had,
> The devil to him did appear,
> And offer'd him his service fair.
> In sooth right well he served his will,
> Whatever he might order still,
> And never did he once despair,
> Though lugg'd right often by the hair.
> He tranquilly put up with all,
> Until one day it did befall,
> All dark and gloomy grew the sky,
> And down came torrents from on high.
> 'Tis terror of such rain to tell ;
> Right lucky to whose lot it fell
> Beneath a roof to sit or run ;
> But to the devil 'twas no fun,
> For from him quick the clothes they take.
> Hood, mantle off, and no mistake,
> As custom is and law withal,
> And still the same doth ' wisps ' befall.[1]

[1] A " Wisp," *trepaczka*, is a nickname given to grooms from the bunch of rags, &c., with which horses are rubbed down.

And now again that self-same day
The sun his beauty doth display,
Sends forth his brilliant rays of light ;
'Twas warm, 'twas beautiful and bright.
Each gentleman without delay
His mantle on his groom doth lay ;
Wet was the mantle, full of rain ;
Then first it did the devil pain.
Himself he did unto his lord
Reveal, and thus he spoke the word :
' Here is no place for me to dwell,
To you, my lord, I bid farewell.
By trial this I've learnt for sure,
That wisps an evil life endure,
Where'er they turn, where'er they be,
They're entertain'd with misery.'

   Of what then boast ?   The way you fare,
Thou seest, the devil could not bear ;
And that is surely token sound,
A life that's worse cannot be found,
Than that to which ye wisps submit.
But when I do with scholars sit—
I do not boast, I but recount—
Town children to a great amount,
Entrusted to my watchful eyes,
I with the rod do oft chastise,
Thus cure of mine own beatings gain—
On feast-days I've no fear of pain.
But when the time of Lent is near,
To me right welcome and right dear,
Whereof the tale were lengthy all,

What solace then doth me befall!
When I am in the country far,
Then all things to my liking are;
Then naught of poverty I know,
I feel right jolly as I go.
When to a village I draw near,
The dogs are in a state of fear,
If one perchance to bark turns back,
My stick to smite him is not slack.
The farmers' wives observe me nigh,
And scuttle up right graciously;
They show no laziness at all,
Down on their knees at once they fall,
My images they kiss with glee,
And many a gift they promise me;
Each smites with energy her breast,
And asks what gift will please me best.
I ask an egg; to aid my need
She's to the basket off with speed,
She searches all the hen-roosts round,
She climbs where'er a nest is found,
All corners scans with anxious heart,
Lets me not empty-handed part.
Then off I go with merriment,
For eggs I've to my heart's content;
And if a hen I chance to meet,
Or if a goose or duck I greet,
If I once hold upon it lay,
To school it goes with me away;
The farmer may with anger burn,
Yet dare say nothing in return,

> No, not an angry word, lest he
> To Passau's court should cited be."

The dispute becomes more and more vehement and ends in a regular fight, engaged in which the writer leaves the worthy pair and takes himself off, concluding with some sententious remarks on home as compared with a public-house.

It will perhaps be most interesting if I close my account of the Bohemian poetical literature of the fourteenth century with a translation of about two-thirds of the extant portion of a ballad on the death of the blind King of Bohemia, John of Luxembourg, in the battle of Creçy. Several strings of names occur in the latter part of the poem, so that I have not thought it worth while to translate the whole of the extant fragment, which is preserved by Prokop Lupacz, commonly called Lupacius, in his history of the Emperor Charles IV. published at Prague in 1584.

DEATH OF KING JAN.

"Young Klimberk!" briefly said the King,
"Thy noble sire to mem'ry bring,
'Gainst whom no charge of ill was brought,
But much the good that he hath wrought.
Thou art thyself a gallant knight,

Young, brave, and ripe for vent'rous fight,
I know thou'lt lead me not away,
I trust thou'lt lead me to the fray,
Where I my sword in fight shall try."
"Have thou no care!" he made reply,
" As thou hast said, so shall it be,
Thy pleasure shall be done for thee.
God for thy soul entreat this day,
And spur thy steed! there lies our way,
Where we'll as friends each other greet,
When on the judgment day we meet ! "
    E'en as the word, so is the deed;
Lord Henry after him doth speed,
With him there rushes to the fight
Full many an honourable knight,
His war-cry shouting loud and bold ;
Each in his heart this thought doth hold,
That when a man his lord is near,
No mortal harm hath he to fear.
    The enemy is smit with dread,
When wide the Vulture's wings are spread,[1]
Beneath them that belovèd knight,
Shouting his war-cry " Prague," in sight.
Into the thickest of the foes
As arrow swift he dauntless goes,
And vehemently doth he swing
Those golden bells of pleasant ring,
Wherewith he wont his steed incite,
When bold he mounteth him for fight ;

---

[1] The Vulture was the device on the banner of the king.

And many a knightly deed did he,
Right woeful to the enemy,
And many a stroke he struck that day,
Through armour strong that made a way ;
Both horse and man right valiant were,
And with both hands he did not spare,
But smote as one in frenzy fit ;
Whate'er, where'er by him was hit,
Was all to-broken and to-hewn,
And fragments on the ground were strewn.
    Seeing his vent'rous valour free,
Bolder and bolder needs must be
All those, who in his company
Their lord's right valiant deeds did see.
They charged upon the enemies
With weapons sharp in knightly wise,
Right hon'rably themselves they bore,
With sword, with dagger evermore
They hew'd, they stabb'd with all their force ;
Blood stream'd from flank of ev'ry horse,
They struck their spurs so deeply in,
For 'twas their will the field to win
Or else to better worlds to rise.
    Here the red Rose [1] in blooming guise
All brightly show'd its ruby sheen ;
Splendid within its heart was seen
Gleaming with pure Arabian gold,
'Neath which a knightly warrior bold
Deep paths did through the foemen hew,

_____
[1] The device of the Lord of Rosenberg.

E'en as becomes a hero true.
To no man yielding gave he way,
That place to gain did still essay,
Where he such knightly deed might do,
It might be held in mem'ry true.
And should the question asked be,
Good people might with conscience free,
From time to time, from year to year,
Relate it ever without fear,
While the true Rose should blossom nigh
The Lion,[1] as in time gone by.
　　Here too the golden Wheel[2] shone bright,
'Neath which did never youthful knight
Such hard adventure, hero-wise,
As noble Klimberk, enterprise ;
Who, naught regarding jeopardy,
Did serve his lord right faithfully.
On sire and grandsire well he thought,
And woe unto the foemen brought,
Where'er himself he turn'd in strife,
He smote, hew'd, stabb'd, and reft of life !

　*　　　*　　　*　　　*　　　*

A tradition respecting the behaviour of King Edward III. of England after this battle appears to have been preserved in Bohemia, and is thus recorded by the chronicler Hajek in 1541, who, however, I must admit,

---

[1] The Lion with two tails is the emblem of Bohemia.
[2] The device of the Klimberk family.

is not a very trustworthy witness to more than the mere existence of the tradition. Hajek says : " And when that battle was ended and the King of England saw that his enemies were all fled and gone, he rode in person to view the slain ; and being informed that the King of Bohemia had also perished there, he commanded his body to be diligently sought for, and when he saw him lying dead amongst others, he dismounted from his horse, and lifted him up with his own hands, saying to him very sorrowfully : ' O dear King of Bohemia, thou oughtest to have had another couch than be lying here on the ground ; ' and forthwith he commanded him to be taken thence and carried into his own army, and his armour to be taken off.   And he commanded his body to be laid out honourably and conveyed to Luxembourg, and to be honourably buried there in the Abbey of the Virgin Mary, where are brethren of the order of St. Benedict." It is quite possible that this account may have been derived from the lost portion of the ballad the first part of the remaining fragment of which I have translated above.

III.

HE fourteenth century is the era of the rise of Bohemian prose. Its first beginnings were simple and inconspicuous enough. Following the order of Erben's "Výbor z Literatury Czeské," we come first to the "Book of the Old Lord of Rosenberg." This is more valuable to the legal antiquary than to the student of literature. Only extracts are given by Erben, but it is printed entire with a Latin translation in A. Kucharski's "Pomniki Pravodawstwa Slowianskiego" (Warsaw, 1838). As it is the earliest relic of Bohemian prose, I give one or two extracts just to exhibit its nature.

"XIII. HOW TO CITE A VAGABOND.

"58. It is the law to cite a vagabond at three markets.

When anyone is cited to Prague as a vagabond, it is the law to cite him at the first market, then it is the law to cite him at a second market in the town, where he has obtained the beadle from the inferior office to cite him with him. Then both beadles together have to cite him together at a third market in the district, in which lies the town nearest adjoining to the inferior office."

" 59. If a vagabond is cited, it is the law to cite him conscientiously at markets, and by the same law as other people who have houses are cited, but for this reason he is cited at three markets, because a vagabond has nowhere any house or property, only he wanders, because he is not settled, and therefore he is not cited from anywhere."

" XV.   An Abbot.

" 63. It is the law to cite an abbot by beadles in the monastery, and afterwards to complete his citation as a bachelor in a case of inheritance. When an abbot is cited for anything, it is the law to cite the abbot first, the prior by name second, the provost or cellarer (*klucznik*, key-bearer) by name third, and moreover to say : ' and the whole convent.' "

" 64. It is the law to cite an abbess who presides over nuns as an abbot or provost."

Some of the rules, by which citations served at the houses of the persons to be cited were governed, are worth noticing, for instance :—

" 35. When the beadles cite, and they are told the lady is at mass or at a banquet or on a visit, the citation is legally performed ; it is not invalid, because she will soon return home, and the household is at home."

" 38. If the beadle meets the lady travelling with the lord on the highway, he has no right to serve a citation, but always in the mansion where she resides and dwells."

In a manuscript written about the middle of the fourteenth century are found several prose legends, from which I have selected the united legends of St. Cyril, St. Methodius and St. Ludmilla of Bohemia, passing over those of saints more or less common to Christendom.

" When the Almighty Lord willed that through the bright beams of his Holy Spirit the Christian faith should spread itself throughout all the world, then in those times, in which the reverend master St. Augus-

tine[1] was alive and flourished in the world, there arose
a godly man by name Quirillus, who went into that
country which hight Bulgaria, and converted the
people to the Christian faith; and afterwards he went
into Moravia and converted the Moravian people also
to God. But because the people of those times were dull
towards the service of God, the holy Quirillus bethought
himself by help of the Holy Spirit to organize the
service of God in the Slavonic tongue, and translated
all the scriptures of the old and new law; and this
order holds in Slavonic countries even unto the present
day. Afterwards the holy Quirillus, leaving in Moravia
his brother, who was named Methodius, went to Rome
for devotion; and there the holy father, the pope, and
other wise men reproved the holy Quirillus for that he
had ordained to chant the service of God in Slavonic.
To whom the holy Quirillus excused himself, saying,
' Every spirit ought to praise God in every tongue.
And since the Lord hath ordained the Slavonic tongue
as well as other languages, as the Lord put it into my

[1] Probably a confusion between Augustine of Hippo and the
Augustine who converted the English. So that the anachronism
is not quite so glaring as at first sight.

mind, so have I by this act converted many wanderers to the holy faith.' Hearing this and admiring his firm faith, they confirmed and ordained that the service of God should be chanted in these countries even unto this day, of which confirmation the holy Quirillus obtained letters from the holy father the pope, and sent them into these countries, and afterwards he entered into the spiritual order and died serving God diligently. But his brother Metudius, who had remained in Moravia, was made archbishop by the king of Moravia, whose name was Swatopluk, and had under him seven other bishops. In those times the land of Bohemia was still in error of faith and worshipped pagan idols. And then there was a celebrated woman of natural genius, but a witch, by name Libussa, by whose ordinance the city of Prague was founded. And afterwards when the Bohemians elected prince a peasant ploughman, but a very wise man, by name Przemysl, then they gave Libussa in marriage to him ; from which source hath come the lineage of Bohemian princes and kings famous throughout the whole world even unto this day. Afterwards, after many years, there came from this source a duke of Bohemia, by name

Borzivoj, a kindly man, of goodly stature, full of wisdom; he took unto himself for lady of his land the daughter of Slavnik, of the district of Melnik, by name Ludmilla; she in her youth also worshipped pagan idols.   And when, once upon a time, the Bohemian duke Borzivoj went to the royal court of Swatopluk, in Moravia, the king gave him a welcome and invited him to dinner; but allowed him not to sit among the Christians, saying, ' According to pagan custom it appertaineth to thee to sit on the floor in front of the table.'   On whom the Archbishop Metudius took compassion, and being ashamed for him, saith unto him : ' Eh ! being so great a prince, art thou not ashamed that thou art thrust away from an honourable seat, and on account of the idols of thy erroneous faith sittest dishonourably upon the ground ? '   ' What matters it ? ' he replied ; ' for what doth your Christian faith avail ? '   To whom the holy Metudius saith, ' If thou wouldst, thou couldst well better this : renounce thy devilish idols, and thou wilt be a lord over thy lords, and wilt subdue all thine enemies beneath thy power, and thy posterity will come gloriously to might; for there is a prophecy prophesied long ago concerning the Bohemian princes.' To whom the duke saith, 'If this be so, why dost thou not christen me at once? or what hindereth?' The holy Metudius saith, 'Naught hindereth us, only be ready to believe with constant heart in God the Father Almighty, and in his Son Jesus Christ, and in the Holy Spirit, who is the enlightener of all faithful souls; and this do, not only from desire of temporal prosperity, but for the salvation of body and soul and abiding with God for ever.' Hearing this holy speech, the Bohemian prince by the strengthening of the Holy Spirit earnestly desired the archbishop to christen him. And on the morrow the holy father Metudius, seeing the constant desire of the prince, christened him, with thirty servants who had come with him. Then, having confirmed himself in the holy faith, he took with him a priest, whose name was Kaïk, and returned to Bohemia, and caused a church to be built in the name of the holy Clement, above the castle which is called Gradist, and made that priest minister thereof. And meanwhile the land of Bohemia abundantly accepted the holy faith. Not many days afterwards the holy father Metudius came into Bohemia and christened the holy Ludmilla with many others, whereby

the holy faith spread itself mightily in the land of
Bohemia. The devil, seeing a multitude of souls libe-
rating themselves from his power, excited the Bohemian
lords against the priests, and that faithful prince was
driven out of the land of Bohemia on account of the
Christian faith. Wherefore he immediately arose and
went to King Swatopluk and the Bishop Metudius in
Moravia, and there being by them honourably received
spent some time with them. But since the spite of
human cunning, though it flourisheth for a time, cannot endure long, the older lords in the land of Bohemia
recalled their duke back again with honour, and he on
his return built a church in the name of the Holy Queen
in the city of Prague, as he had vowed to the Mother
of God in his exile in Moravia. This godly man was
of the first princes of the land of Bohemia who founded
houses of God, and appointed priests with clergy and
with spiritual persons for the service of God. And
afterwards he had three sons and three daughters by
his holy lady Ludmilla, according as the holy father
Metudius had prophesied to him, that his children were
to be born in all that was good. And meanwhile Duke
Borzivoj spent his days in great honour, and departed

after commending himself to God, and in his stead his son Sbyhniew received the principality of Bohemia. He also, even as his father, established churches and priests and gloriously exalted the Christian faith, and departed, and Wratislaw, father of the holy Wenceslaw, was prince in Bohemia in his stead; and he built a convent in the Castle of Prague in the name of St. George for spiritual damsels. Meanwhile the holy Ludmilla, after the death of her lord, remained in purity even unto her end, serving God diligently, keeping under her body by fasts, kneeling, prayers, and various doings, in charitable works for the sake of the Lord, lovingly nourishing the poor, priests, and pilgrims, giving alms to the sick and prisoners, to the suffering and needy, so that she may be called a shining star that illuminated all the land of Bohemia with the bright beams of her holy example. And as the holy Ludmilla had in her guardianship her grandson, the holy Wenceslas, her daughter-in-law, a merciless pagan, envying this, wickedly bethought her in her heart how to destroy the holy Ludmilla, and turn that holy child, the holy Wenceslas, to pagan idols, and meanwhile extirpate the Christians in the land of Bohemia; even as she afterwards attempted this, driving the priests out of the land and commanding the church doors everywhere to be fastened up. The holy Ludmilla observing this migrated to the Castle of Tetin, and there, after receiving the whole sacrament,[1] commended her soul to the Lord. And in that same hour two merciless executioners, sent for her death, broke open the doors of her chamber, and without any shame began insultingly to drag away their gracious princess. To whom she said, ' What do ye ? have ye forgotten what good I have done you ?' This said the noble saint, grieving more for their sin than for the loss of her own life ; but paying no regard thereto, they put a cord round her holy neck and began to strangle her. To whom she said, as she best could, ' Rather cut off my head, that rolling in my blood for the sake of my Jesus Christ, I may obtain the crown of the holy martyrs.' Paying no regard thereto, the merciless executioners encompassed her holy neck and strangled her, and angels took her soul and carried it to the joy of heaven. And afterwards many holy wonders were wrought through the holy Ludmilla

[1] Probably an allusion to communion in both kinds, according to the custom of the Greek Church.

upon various people, and are wrought even unto the present day. And some years afterwards the holy Wenceslas brought her holy body from Tetin to Prague, and buried it honourably at St. George's, in the convent of the spiritual damsels."

Part of the Scriptures—for instance, the Gospels and Psalter—were translated into Bohemian as early as the tenth century, but the whole Bible does not appear to have been translated before the fourteenth century; at any rate no manuscripts of earlier date are known. There exists also a Life of Christ, apparently from an unknown Latin prototype, carefully composed in accordance with the four Gospels, and only in one place referring to the apocryphal Gospel of Nicodemus. The writer has, however, allowed himself a good deal of licence in filling up the outlines of the Gospel history. I give a specimen:—

" (85.) And when Jesus came that evening to Bethany, his mother came out weeping to meet him, and embraced him lovingly. Afterwards she sat down with him to supper. Here his mother ate more tears than food, neither did she do aught else but gaze continually into his face. That evening Jesus spake openly

to the apostles, how he was to be sold and betrayed
to death. O, bitter supper of thine, dear mother, when
thou didst hear such news! Here saith St. Anselm:
If the Mother of God could have known who was about
to betray her son, she would have taken a rope upon
her neck and fallen on the ground before him weeping,
and saying, ' Dear Judas, have pity on me, unhappy
woman! If thou desirest of me a cup of money, I will
gladly work for thee with my hands all my days, and
give thee all my wages.   If that is not enough, sell
me to some one without injury to my honour, and en-
slave me somewhere in service, only have pity upon
me, and betray not my dear son! '   And Anselm saith
likewise, that had she seen the betrayer of her son she
would have wept so piteously before him, that even
had he been more hard-hearted than the devil she
would have brought him to compassion.   The Son of
God would not therefore reveal this to her, lest that
should have been broken up by her which had been
written respecting his passion for the salvation of the
whole world ; but he looked at her that evening and
comforted her with these words, saying, ' Weep not
dear mother! I shall remain with thee all day to-

morrow.' That night Jesus was at Bethany, conversing graciously with his mother and disciples, but Judas was not there, but was already on the way to compass his death."

Among the works of the celebrated Albertus Magnus (ob. 1280), who was bishop of Ratisbon from 1260 to 1262, a high place is held by the "Paradise of the Soul" or "Book of the Virtues." In the fourteenth century this work was freely translated, or rather imitated and enlarged, by an anonymous Bohemian writer, so that the forty-two chapters of the original have become sixty-two in the translation. I give as a specimen part of chapter xx., "Of Truth," which will exhibit the principles inculcated by the literary men of Bohemia :—

" Truth is sure and faithful, when heart, mouth, and actions are in unison. For whoso has one thing in his heart and another in his mouth, and fulfils not by deeds what he speaks with his mouth, that man is not truthful. As the Lord himself saith in the Gospel : 'Not every one that saith unto me twice, Lord ! Lord ! will enter into the kingdom of heaven.' That is to say, whoso only speaks with his mouth and holds faith in his heart, and fulfils it not by deed, that man is not faithful and will not enter into the kingdom of heaven. As saith St. Paul: Be followers of me, and follow those people who teach with the heart, with the mouth, and by their works. That man is faithful and sure who fulfils what he promises to God and to men, without any alteration, save if he alters his promise for something better, as the heavenly king sometimes alters his judgment over sinful men, when they repent. As it was altered for King Ezekias, whom he had informed by the holy Esaias the prophet, that he must die, but afterwards for his weeping and for his prayer added to him fifteen years; and he had announced by Jonas to the great city of Nineveh destruction after forty days, but afterwards forgave them. It may incline us to the love of truth, that our dear Lord names himself the Truth, saying, 'I am the way and the truth; and whoso loveth the truth walketh in the light of God.' For truth is the light of our soul, and truth is the countenance of God. And therefore whoso hath more of truth and loveth truth, is like to good money, which hath good silver and a good image. Likewise falsehood is the countenance of the devil; therefore a false man is like money which has a fair image but bad silver; so also a false man hath a fair countenance and an evil life. And as a hundred bad coins are not worth one good one, so likewise a hundred false men are not worth one good one. Firm truth is the rule of the whole life, and indicator of all good actions; and whoso loveth the truth hath a fair mouth and tongue; and likewise the false man defileth his mouth more with falsehood than if it were full of filthy worms, in the eyes of the soul and of good people, to whom falsehood is very disgusting; for good and pure men have a life of righteousness, and their life is not counter to truth, and their deeds and works are faithful and true. And therefore true men love truth also in others. For everybody associateth himself to another according to his works—the faithful to the faithful, the good to the good, the wicked to the wicked, and that because each loveth that which is like himself. And therefore he who is faithful would be glad if all were faithful, that therein they might be like him. It may incline us to truth that it conquers all things. For everything changes, but truth never; as saith the Lord himself in the Gospel, 'Heaven and earth can be changed rather than my words.'"

This will perhaps be a sufficient specimen of a work which partakes more or less of the nature of a translation, however free, and with whatever additions it may have been enlarged. We come now to works, written originally in Latin in Bohemia, and translated either by the original writer or a contemporary hand into the native language. Such are both the " Chronicle of Pulkava " and the " Autobiography of the Emperor Charles IV."

Pribik or Pribislaw, of Hradcin, surnamed Pulkava, was first of all a notary of the Archbishop of Prague, then director of the collegiate school of St. Giles at Prague, and finally from the year 1378 rector of Chudenice, where he died in 1380. He wrote a Bohemian chronicle originally in the Latin language, which in the year 1374, at the special request of the Emperor Charles IV., he corrected and enlarged by interweaving some important documents and an old chronicle of the land of Brandenburg, which had then just been united to Bohemia. Later still, it appears that he translated it into the Bohemian language himself. As the Latin is undoubtedly the original, I give but a brief specimen of the work:—

" Chapter LXXV.

"How King Przemysl by the faithlessness of his lords was slain in Austria, and of other matters.

" In the year of the Lord 1278, King Otakar, being sorry that he had given up those lands (Austria, Styria, and Carinthia), and being craftily encouraged and instigated by some dishonourable counsellors of his, determined to have them back again, or give his life for it. Therefore, collecting an army, he invaded Austria, and laid it waste with fire and rapine. Without moving from the district of Lawen, he stood some days in the open field, and then marched to the town of Drosendorf, and pitched his camp there. Rudolf, learning this, and crossing the Danube with his army, posted himself on the frontiers of Moravia; when Otakar too had come to a hill in a wood near unto the river Morava, knowing nought certain concerning the King of the Empire.[1] Therefore, by the instigation of that dishonourable and faithless villain, Milota, he

[1] It must be remembered that Rudolf of Hapsburg was never crowned Emperor by the Pope, and was therefore only King of the Romans.

(Rudolf) sent spies to ascertain how it was there; for
this Milota, a dishonourable scoundrel, had some old
anger in his heart against the king, although the king
had made him lord and ruler in all Moravia. Thus
then, when the King of the Empire, day after day, by
the contrivance of this traitorous Milota, perceived
King Otakar with his men in security, and when he
had made himself strong with his own men, he sud-
denly approached, and with speed surrounded the
army. King Otakar seeing the large army of the King
of the Empire, and observing that many dishonourable
traitors had joined it, of whom he had been formerly
warned by the King of the Empire, because he had
been brought up at his court, paid no regard thereto,
but drew his army together; and thus, not waiting for
the main body of his people, nor having any evil sus-
picion of Milota, committed himself to the chances of
battle, having hope to obtain victory, and boldly determined to fight. Thus when the armies met on both
sides, they began to fight with a good will; but meanwhile, on a sudden, that dishonourable traitor Milota,
forgetting the many benefactions of the king, withdrew
with his men from his king and lord. In such an evil

moment of this battle did the wicked traitors dishonourably flee. Then took place a great and very
hard battle, when some of the Bohemians fell to the
ground, and others fled from their king. Wherefore
the king was there defeated and slain in that battle, on
the day of St. Rufus; and the King of the Empire
mourned his death greatly. Thus, then, the king was
carried to Prague, and buried honourably in Prague;
and his son Wenceslas reigned in his stead, being only
five years old, a young child; and the Margrave of
Brandenburg took charge of him, as a powerful
guardian, as his father had appointed.

"This year, John, Bishop of Prague, died, and
Tobias, the five-and-twentieth bishop, became bishop
in his stead.

"In these times the land of Bohemia was very ill-
governed, for many Saxons and other Germans invaded
the land, and so terribly harassed the Bohemians
that many fled from their houses, and lived in the
forests. Wherefore, because they ploughed not the
lands, there was great hunger in the land; and, from
the cruelty of those Germans, the land was greatly injured, and many churches, too, were destroyed. And

this continued thus until the lords took counsel with the Margrave of Brandenburg, and intrusted the government of the land to the Bishop Tobias ; and so the Saxons and other Germans were driven out of the land, and the people were freed from their oppressions."

The Emperor Charles IV. appears to have written his autobiography in Latin, for the instruction of his successors on both thrones—that of Bohemia and that of the Empire—in the year 1363, beginning with his birth in 1316, and ending with the year 1346, when he was elected King of the Romans. It was translated into Bohemian in the fourteenth century, and, apparently, not long after its appearance in Latin. Unfortunately, a considerable portion is lost, and has been supplied by an inferior pen. Both as a historical and as a literary document, the value of this autobiography is very great ; but as it is not altogether an original Bohemian work, I shall content myself with a brief extract from chapter xiv. :—

" At this time, when our father had lost one eye, he began to feel weakness in the other, and went incognito to physicians at Montpellier, to see whether he could be cured ; nevertheless he, at this time (1340), became blind. And at this time we were going to the aid of the King of Spain, against the King of Granada, and had already sent on our people and armaments through Agace to Montalban; but our father detained us at Montpellier, secretly preventing us from going further. And when our father could not be cured, we went with him to Pope Benedict XII., at Avignon, to negotiate with him about the Peter's pence, which are paid in the bishopric of Breslau. But that was not arranged then, but remained in dispute. But afterwards the dispute was settled, which there was between the Church of Rome and the aforesaid bishopric for the aforesaid money. But when we were there, we confessed to the Pope concerning the vision which we had had about the Delfin of Vienne,[1] when we were in Italy, as is aforesaid. But at that time it seemed to us to be better to keep silence, for several reasons, than to reveal and relate it to our father. And when we were with the Pope, Peter, Cardinal of the holy

---

[1] From whom the Dauphin of France obtained his title. Charles had seen him struck by an angel in a dream on horseback in the midst of his army, and he was actually killed in that very position by a shot from a crossbow.

H

martyrs Nereus and Achilles, of whom mention has
previously been made, since he celebrated mass on
Ash Wednesday, as has been afore related, entertained
us in his house, we being at that time Margrave of
Moravia, when we were staying with Pope Benedict.
He said to us on one occasion, when he was with us in
his house, ' Thou wilt yet be King of the Romans.'
We answered him, ' Thou wilt first be Pope.'   And
both these things came to pass, as will be related
below." [1]

The coronation service of the King of Bohemia was
originally drawn up in Latin by the Emperor Charles
IV., and was afterwards translated into Bohemian.
The following brief extract may be interesting,
as showing the originally elective nature of the
Crown :—

"Then shall the archbishop say, with moderated
and solemn voice, ' Wilt thou hold, and by righteous
actions preserve the Christian faith given by Christian
men ?'

" Answer : ' I will.'

" Again he shall ask him : ' Wilt thou govern and

[1] Peter de Rosières was afterwards Pope Clement VI.

defend the kingdom intrusted to thee by God, according to the righteousness of thy ancestors ?'

" Answer : ' As, being strengthened by the Divine aid and the comfort of all his faithful ones, I shall be able, so do I promise all faithfully to do.'

" Then shall the archbishop speak to the people in these words : ' Will ye also submit yourselves to N. as prince and ruler, and be obedient to his command, according to the word of the holy Apostle, who saith, Let every soul be subject to the higher powers, whether to the king as supreme ?'

" Then shall it be said by the clergy and people standing round with one voice : ' Willingly, willingly, willingly.' "

The rules of practice of the tribunal of the realm (*ordo judicii terræ*) were originally drawn up in Latin, between 1348 and 1355, in two recensions, and afterwards in Bohemian, but in a very free translation, which sometimes abridges, sometimes enlarges, and sometimes altogether alters the original. Like the book of the old Lord of Rosenberg, it is the work of a contemporary writer, but not of a legislator, and it therefore never had any legal validity ; still it exhibits

for us not only the practice of the tribunals, but also
many principles of law which were formerly observed
in Bohemia, and thus belongs to the class of the most
important records of mediæval jurisprudence, both in
Slavonic countries in particular and Europe in general.

When I read the earlier part of this work for the
first time, I found myself transported to the great
appeal of Bolingbroke *versus* Mowbray, in Shakespeare's " Richard II.," so similar are both the forms
and principles of procedure. As that carries us
only up to the conflict, which is put an end to by the
intervention of the king, I shall select my specimens
from the description of the conflict itself and the sub-
sequent proceedings.

" (22.) And when the appointed time comes, then
the appellant, being ready for battle, must take his
oath first, as the lords shall give him the formula.
And if he makes an error in the oath, then shall he
lose his cause. If then he gets through in his oath,
then the appealed, being also ready for battle, must
swear to his innocence. If he makes an error in the
oath, then shall he lose his cause and his life. And if
he gets through, then shall they forthwith fight with-

out armour, only in tunics and hose, with swords and behind shields, in lists prepared for them, as is the custom.

" (23.) Here mark that from time immemorial this was the rule : If the appealed made error in the oath, and did not rectify it after three attempts, he should lose both his cause and his head. In contravention of this, from favour, the lords determined for one in the time of the late emperor that he was not to be beheaded immediately for that oath, but lost his cause, and the appellant gained his. But instead of being beheaded, the appealed is to be put into perpetual prison, that the Burggrave of Prague do keep him until death, as is right for a prisoner; and if the Burggrave of Prague be his relative by birth, then he must be put into other ward, where it seemeth good to the king and the lords of the land, and there he is to be kept as is right for a prisoner, until the king and the lords of the land shall have fully ascertained his innocence, or until the appellant and his friends have released him from guilt and entreated the king and the lords for him that he may be released.

" (24.) And if one of the twain dare not fight, before

he enters into the lists he must entreat the lords to grant him a conference with the Burggrave of Prague; which Burggrave must accompany him safely for three miles from the castle of Prague, so that he may escape from the violence of his enemies.

"(25.) But if they have both entered into the lists and have begun to fight, and if one of them be wearied, he must ask for a respite, and must be hearkened to therein. Then the Burggrave of Prague must place between them a pole, that neither may reach at the other over it for the space of an hour; which pole two officials, a beadle and a judge, must hold in readiness, and should either desire it, it must be ready thrice for a respite, and always for the space of an hour.

" (26.) And if one overcome the other, then must he cut off his head, and place his head between his feet; unless a better arrangement has been come to between them with the king's will and the assent of the lords. And when he has beheaded him and placed his head between his feet, then must he kneel on one knee and thank the king and the lords for right justice, and place two hellers (coins) upon him, and present him with them. And thus he is victorious over him, and ob-tains justice in the cause. And this must be entered for him in the records, that no relative may avenge him. If then any one doth avenge him, that man shall forfeit life and goods to the king's majesty and all the lords, and never shall he or his children enjoy the benefit of the tribunal of the land."

Then (27 and 28) come rules of procedure in case the appealed person is afraid to fight, or does not appear on the appointed day.

" (29.) If then all this be done and the appealed does not come to terms with the appellant and the officials, then must the appellant, wherever he finds the appealed, take or slay him, and fastening a billet of wood to him, must tie him by the feet to a horse's tail, without taking off any of his clothes, and drag him under the gallows at Prague. And he must inform the officials, and take an officer of the court to view him. And when the officer has acknowledged it, he must enter it in the records, and no man must avenge him.

" (30.) Here mark, that if the appealed be found with his wedded wife, and she embrace him or conceal him with her dress, he may not be taken from her nor suffer any harm. And, likewise, if he be by the tomb of St. Wenceslas in the Cathedral at Prague, or in the presence of the Queen of Bohemia, he may not be taken, but may enjoy quiet."

" (37.) If a burgess appeal a peasant, they must do battle with clubs and great shields, for they are both of the serf order, and it has been ordained from time immemorial that for such battle they must not use swords."

"(40.) If a widow appeal one of equal nobility with herself for the homicide of her husband or any relative, she must proceed against the appealed in the same manner as a man.   If then she shall have to do battle with him, then must the appealed stand in a shaft dug in the ground up to the girdle, with a sword and a great shield, and in that shaft turn himself as best he can and defend himself against her.   And she must also be with a sword and a shield in circular lists prepared for the purpose.   And neither may he go out of the shaft nor she out of the lists until one has overcome the other.   If then one of them goes out, he loses his right.   And a maiden of eighteen years old or older, if she wishes to do battle thus with her enemy, may enjoy the same right."

We come now to the work of a great lawyer, written originally in the Bohemian tongue, the "Exposition of the Common Law of the Land of Bohemia," by Andrew of Dubá. The office of Chief Justice in Bohemia was held from 1343 to 1394 by Andrew of Dubá, who resigned it in the latter year, but lived eighteen years afterwards, still taking part in the grand assizes of the realm. This appearing to be a very long space of time for one and the same person, Dr. F. Palacky conjectured that it was not one person, but two—a father and son, the former of whom was Chief Justice till 1361, and the latter till 1394. If this conjecture be correct, the work under consideration must have proceeded from the pen of the latter, and that probably, according to Erben, about the year 1400. To a foreigner, and also in a literary point of view, the dedicatory address to King Wenceslas IV. is the most interesting portion of the whole. This begins :—

" To the most illustrious prince and lord, the lord Wenceslas, monarch of the Romans and King of Bohemia, my most gracious lord and inheritor by birth of the Crown of Bohemia; I, Andrew the elder of Dubá, present my humble service ready for obedience

to Thy Majesty.   Herein, as Thy faithful servant and
by natural fealty a subject of Thy Crown of Bohemia,
for Thy honour and Thy renown and that of the whole
land of Bohemia, and for the common good, I have
written down my recollections, which I have heard
from my forefathers and from many aged lords who
have loved the common law (*právo, jura*) of the land of
Bohemia, and have myself, being many years in the
office of chief justice, in the time of Thy father and
Thyself, learned, conducted, and held it faithfully, with
my faithful associates and other officials of that day ;
principally in order that Thy honoured memory and the
order of the land may not be impaired through me,
aged man that I am.   For I think that there are few
of the Bohemian lords who remember what their
fathers held for law; and not remembering or knowing, they also direct their minds and thoughts according to their own will in their offices, harshly obtaining
money, contrary to ancient ordinance.   And through
this the Crown of Bohemia is hindered and injured,
mainly in the service of knights and gentlemen, Thou
in Thy monarchy, the community of persons spiritual
and lay in honour and wealth, the poor and orphans in

their inheritance, and the common law of Bohemia in its order. And against whom is the common outcry but against Thee? Against whom is complaint to God, but against Thee? Of whom is there an evil memory but of Thee? Thou canst easily rid Thyself of this and not be guilty thereof, only receive instruction and do thine endeavour; command those, to whom Thou shalt give or hast given offices and takest an oath from them, to practise the truth of God, in that truth and to that truth exercising the ancient common law without invention of new rules of right. Not therein to seek for money, contrary to ancient ordinance; within that ordinance to do mercy, and not to be partial, being always ready for each man according to his need, for it is for that that they receive and hold. Likewise command that they summon not people before themselves for their own matters; likewise that their deputies keep not people's agents with them, who conduct lawsuits and privily take counsel with them. Command likewise that they attend to Thy rightful escheats according to law; that, where Thou or any one in Thy stead is rightly entitled, they neglect him not; that, where Thou art not rightly en-

titled, there be forthwith for the sake of Thy reputation
a final sentence pronounced upon Thy claim, that it may
be satisfied in law. Likewise, above all, put a stop to
outcry in the court of justice of the country on account
of Thy officials. For where an official excuses his lord,
and does not excuse himself by means of his lord, it is
good; but where the official says, ' That isn't through
me,' and the lord holds his peace, 'tis an ill sign. Therefore because Thou art the pillar and light of all justice
and the punishment of all the bad, beware of the occur-
rence of this through Thy officials. To all the lords Thou
art lord, to all the cunning a sage, to all the unrigh-
teous a snare, to all the good gracious and a very gift
of God.   I say likewise, if Thy sworn officials have
commandment from Thee, and receiving it do not carry
it out in practice as Thou hast commanded, Thou hast
outcry against Thee (as is the case at this day on
account of certain disorders)—command Thy faithful
council to see to this and bring it from worse to better.
Dear lord ! what I write or shall write, that I am not
afraid to speak and proclaim before every man ; for I
do this for no other cause, but for Thy honour and the
common good of the land of Bohemia.

"There are four officers appointed by Thee in the constitution of the land who are called 'chief;' for they are appointed by Thee, the chief lord, chosen and their offices endowed for Thy peace and honour, and that of Thy crown and of all the community of the land of Bohemia, to do right in that which is intrusted to them, first to Thee, and then to poor and rich; and the record of what the lords decide or what people agree to voluntarily is intrusted to them. This they write in books, which are called 'tables' (*dsky*), by their clerks. These lords have or receive their offices from Thee, and make oath to be faithful to Thee and the whole land of Bohemia; from Thee they have honour and wealth, from Thee and from the community they receive a fixed payment for their labour. Three of these must be noble lords: the Burggrave of Prague, the Chief Beadle, and the Chief Justice; but the fourth, the Chief Secretary, must not be a noble lord, but an ordinary man, well educated, and moreover well learned therein. And what each of these has to receive and the distribution of their power, I will write below."

Then follows a description of these officers, their

underlings, their duties and their fees, with various remarks upon their disabilities; and the writer concludes his dedicatory address with the following remarkable words:—

" If Thou wilt be free and clear from the common outcry, and have advantageous thanks from all the community and all the lords together, bid them read this and do thus, and make an ordinance excluding Thy officers from Thy council, and proclaim it to the community while Thou art in health, and Thou wilt be happy in body and in soul. And if Thou wilt hear or bid Thy council to hear, I will point out many an instance in an office where ten kops [1] have been taken instead of one, and a hundred instead of ten; wherefore punish those on account of whom Thou hast outcry against Thee. And if Thou wilt hear me myself, I will tell Thee still more to Thy advantage and honour."

As regards the origin of the Bohemian common law, Andrew of Dubá says :—

" The common law of the land of Bohemia is of ancient date, even from the time of paganism, and principally from the ploughman Przemysl and from

[1] A kop is a sum of 60 groschen.

those lords who lived at that time. And of this there is certain proof; for many pagan customs are retained in it, as purgation by hot iron or casting into water. And this custom stood without interruption to the time of the Emperor Charles and the priest Arnost, first archbishop of Prague."

He proceeds to divide the judicial system of Bohemia into three grand divisions, the *Súd dvorsky,* or "Court tribunal," corresponding to the old Court of Exchequer with us, the spiritual tribunals, and the *zemské pravo svobodné,* the "free common law of the land," corresponding to the courts of King's Bench and Common Pleas. Everybody, he says, is bound to proceed in due form of law instead of taking the law into his own hands. "But, alas! many leave the law and carry out their own will otherwise. Why so? Only because guilt hath not punishment; and where guilt gets off easily, there evil will is glad to dominate, upon which punishment ought always to be inflicted."

LUDVIK TKADLECZEK and his beloved Adliczka, lived in the first half of the fourteenth century at the court of the widowed Queen Elizabeth, at Königgrätz. Adliczka was the belle of her age, and when she was mar-

ried to another, Tkadleczek (Weaver) commenced his
melancholy lamentations, and immortalized his lady-
love, her beauty, and her virtues, with his pen, which
by a play upon his own name he designated a weaver's
shuttle. This book is very remarkable for the vigour
and flexibility of its language, and also for the amount
of learning and extent of reading displayed in it in the
various arguments of " The Complainer" and " Misfortune," in the course of their long altercation. It
was soon translated into German, and this translation
appears among the earliest productions of the early
German press. I shall give two specimens of this
very original writer, one selected by myself, the other
by the editor of the " Vybor." Adliczka is thus described by Misfortune :—

" She was all good, all honourable, she was worthy
of all honour. For I, Misfortune, was present at her
birth. Happiness was immediately beside her with all
her court, and with her full suite, and with all her
good customs. For they were at once given to her
there and everywhere where she afterwards dwelt.
For that superexcellent, widely renowned queen of
highest race, who is named Honour, sent her mantle,

embroidered with various imperishable flowers, to her
by her highest confidant, whose name is Circumspection. This mantle she adorned with indescribable work,
for it hath never fitted any damsel or dame, save only
her who hath faithfully watched over her honour, according to her rank, without spot, who hath never failed in
point of honour towards God or man ; whereas to each
who has failed in honour, that mantle has been too
short, too strait, and ill-fitting. With that she herself
has clothed all those damsels and dames who have
possessed honour and have been worthy of it before
themselves and before God and before men. She had
also sent her a green wreath, which always kept its
colour, summer and winter, and never, from her youth
up, became sere, faded, or withered, even unto the
married state. And this was brought to her by one
of that queen's damsels, who hight Purity. As an
attendant of the queen on the day when she was born,
I too, Misfortune, was present at all these things, to
see whether she would be committed to me in some
measure, but after waiting long I retired with shame.
I was there when all the court ladies of all Happiness
took her into their fellowship. I was there when she

I

in return promised each of them faithfully to hold true
fellowship with them, each according to her rank.
First to the queen herself, who hight Honour ; to her
she has kept her faith like a woman good and true even
unto the present day.   To Wisdom, to her she holds
unto this day as to her mother.   Modesty, her she
chose for her own special companion.   To Gentleness,
her she obeys and follows as her elder sister.   To
Purity, from her she never strayed till she entered into
the married state.   To Circumspection, to her she committed herself from youth up as to a father.   To Kindness and Friendliness, to them she always clung, and
was always with them, as well among common people
of the lowest and poorest as among people of the
highest rank.   Truth, her she placed in her tablets,
neither will she take her out of her tablets until death.
Sincerity without any mental reserve, of her she took
so fast hold that she will not leave her for anyone.   In
naught did He who created her forget her ; everything
good was collected in her, so that at her baptism who-
ever promised anything for her, stated it honourably
without any hesitation,[1] in every respect.   I, Misfor-

---

[1] This appears to have been looked upon as an omen, corresponding conversely to a *zmatek* or trip in the formula of an oath.

tune, was by her, but not banefully, everywhere on the look-out to see whether she was in aught committed to me; but the Creator himself assigned her a guardian angel, who always watchfully protected her.

* * * * *

" Now the Complainer tells Misfortune that he is the man who has been so cruelly and shamefully separated from his comfort, and by that separation deprived of all comfort in this world.

" ' Ah, ah, Misfortune! I am that unhappy man, I am that person who have been the true and entire servant and true guardian of honour, and ready servant, without aught of indolence, of her of whom thou sayest so much that is noble, so much that is good, so many unheard-of and excellent virtues. I am that Weaver who now address thee, and cry aloud against thee on account of my comfort, on account of all my joy, of which thou hast deprived me. Alas, for thee, and ever alas! Thou hast separated me from her, thou hast separated from me the comforting, the excellent object of my love. She it was with whom I was for several years, and yet meseemeth, as if I had been with her an hour. She it was whom I always endea_ voured to please, and whom I guarded with all my might. She it was who was my teacher, my friend —— all that appertaineth to kindness, that was she to me. She it was who was always with me, and I with her, but now she has removed herself from me. Thou, Misfortune, hast done this evil. She who was my protecting shield against all my earthly adversaries has now quitted me, has left me in orphanhood, and all through thee.' ''

I proceed now finally to give a portion of the extract selected by K. J. Erben to exhibit the beauties and peculiarities of Tkadleczek in the " Výbor," which is certainly a very quaint and curious passage :——

" Now Misfortune replies to the Complainer, and saith, that whatever she has done, she has done well and rightly according to her rule; and not only so, but nothing that is born in the world, be it old man or young, noble or ignoble, learned or illiterate, lay or spiritual, can be without misfortune or escape it, live he as he may.

" The impudent ape went up to the lion while he was sleeping, gave him a slap in the face, and tried to run away; the lion woke up, caught the ape, and pulled off his tail, and now the ape is docked and tailless. The swift hare came to the lion, gave him a nip, and endeavoured to escape; but the lion chased and caught him, took him by the head and pulled his ears, and now the hare has long ears. The cat was playing with the dog and scratched him, and now the dog bears ill will to the cat. Thus art thou also doing, Weaver; thou desirest to assail me, and as it were to over-whelm me with thy harangue, as if thou desiredst to beat me down by force, and as if thou hadst power over me. Beware of me, lest thy skin be torn off. Beware of the anger of the dog, and more than that of the dog. And knowest thou not this, that Solomon saith, that 'A knave or servant subject to his superior may not be above his lord'? Hast thou not heard and read in an epistle of a certain magister, the monk Bernard, who writeth of the order of householders, saying, 'A servant who opposes his lord in his actions and customs, and in his authority, ought not to be kept, but to be driven away evilly and disgracefully, as a present and future evil'? And thinkest thou that I shall sit down by this, that thou being under me, and in my power, and now in my charge, shouldst thus abomin-

ably oppose me? Take care of thy skin, take care of
thy tail, beware of the dog! Know therefore that I
will cut this short, and tell thee aloud that what I have
done with regard to and against thee, I have done
rightly and well. And not only in thy case, but whi-
thersoever I turn in the world, I exhibit my power on
every side, I leave a remembrance behind me. Read
the composition of that wise man, who hight Falis-
thenes, who saith, ' There is naught so mighty upon
earth, whether in wealth or in strength, but that it
sometimes hath adversity or injury from the contrariety
of the world.' And what is the contrariety of the world
but myself, Misfortune, who have been sent forth by
God himself to assail various people with various con-
trarieties, one to-day, another to-morrow? one I have
in my power, another I let go for a time. For this
end was I sent forth, that I might leave no one, either
of high rank; no emperor, king, prince, margrave,
count; or of inferior rank; no honourable, no knight,
squire, gentleman; or of the lowest rank, no citizen,
no peasant; as well in the spiritual order as in the lay;
or in the female sex, without remembrance of me: and
that I might show my power not only on men, but

sometimes also on dumb cattle, and in the case of dumb beasts. Neither do I respect anyone for his high and noble family. Nor do I pass over anyone for the wisdom of his deep thoughts. Neither do I dread any hero, nor feel shame before any philosopher, nor do I spare any beauty; nor is graciousness or un-graciousness, or sorrow, or youth, or age, or aught without my assault; nor childhood, nor youth, nor manhood. And thinkest thou, because thou art in the sphere and condition of early manhood, that thou canst prevail over everything and that everything can be according to thy will? Tell me, Weaver, if thou wilt thus maintain a contrary argument with me, and sayst, that much good has perished from thy comfort through me. Yea, Weaver, hast thou ever read in any books that there was ever any man in the world who was alive after the manner of ordinary nature, that was without my assaults, save only those glorified people and saints who lived by the grace of God above the ordinary custom and above nature? Thou mustest say, that thou hast neither heard nor read of such any-where; thou hast thyself, moreover, never known such a person. How much more fortunate then dost thou

desire to be, that I may honour thee more, than the
Emperor Julius, or the King Alexander, or the excellent, truly excellent, Emperor Charles, at this time
King of Bohemia ? Who, powerful as they were, could
not at times escape my power and my contrariety.
Prithee inquire how many of my misadventures have
happened to those only whom thou knowest, and of
whom thou hast heard in thine own days, whether of
higher or lower rank ; and neither thou nor anyone else
will be able to express in writing or words how many
times this has happened to them. And passing over
all other misadventures, write down only those which
those kings who have been in the land of Hungary
have had from me : there will be no end to them. Ah !
if thou wilt, as thou canst, recollect thine own adversi-
ties only in thine own mind ; how many of them hast
thou also had from me ? For it would have been more
proper to cry out against me about them, or to argue
with me about that which once threatened thy life, thy
property, thy honour, and all the good that thou hadst,
and it would have been convenient to speak of that
rather than of that damsel of thine. Therefore, Weaver,
hold thy peace, speak no more with me of thy darling.

Take me not for so weak a power, think not that I am thine equal, think not that it is as thou thinkest. Know that I rule thee and every man mightily by my power. Thou seest thyself that I pass by nothing, I let nothing pass me without an answer from me. I do as the sun, that shines to the whole world, and is light in itself; to young and old, to Pagan and Jew, to Christian and Greek, to good and bad, to poor and rich alike. Even so there is none of these that has not at some time experienced my assaults. Endure them, likewise, Weaver, according to custom ! "

IV.

N the year 1848 the University of Prague celebrated the 500th anniversary of its foundation by the Emperor Charles IV. In honour of this, its quingentenary, the senate of the University determined to print and publish the first original work of the greatest prose writer that the Czeskish nation had produced, Thomas of Stitný's six books " Of General Christian Matters," a resolution which the circumstances of the times prevented from being carried into execution until 1852, when a handsome octavo volume of 354 pages appeared under the editorship of Karel Jaromir Erben, the Archivarius of Prague. Again in the year 1873 the society called the " Matice Czeská," in honour of the centenary of the birth of one of the greatest names in the late revival of Bohemian literature, Josef Jungmann, the author of perhaps the most wonderful Lexicon ever compiled by a single individual, entrusted Anton Jaroslaw Vrtátko, the librarian of the Bohemian Museum, with the editorship of Thomas of Stitný's "Books of Christian Instruction," which is a fourth edition of the work first mentioned, but with a somewhat different intention, for a different class of readers, and incorporating a number of translations from patristic and mediæval sources.

The first mentioned work was written by Stitný in 1376, primarily for the benefit of his own children, four of whom, three girls and a boy, are represented at the commencement of the manuscript in the University Library at Prague as receiving instruction from his lips, while the second was addressed to his two surviving children, Jan and Anezka, but written for the Bohemian public in general, about 1399, and this is preserved in a manuscript in the possession of the Bohemian Museum. These are the only works of Stitný's that have as yet been printed entire, and for his other great original work, the "Rozmluvy Nábozné," "Religious Conversations," I am dependent on extracts

given in Erben's " Výbor z Literatury Czeské " and
an " Analysis (Rozbor) of Thomas of Stitný's Philo-
sophy " by Professor Hanus, published in 1852. In
1392 Stitný also wrote a series of Sermons for Sundays
and festivals, only extracts from which are printed in the
"Výbor." His first work (1370) was a translation of the
" Soliloquies " of St. Augustine, and he also translated
the Barefooted Friar Hugo's work on the preparation of the heart, Robert Holkot, the Oxford professor,
"De Sapientia Salomonis," the "Summa Virtutum,"
and several other Latin writings of a religious or theo-
logical character.   It is interesting to know, that the
first impulse towards writing received by Stitný came
from one of the great precursors of John Huss, Milicz
of Kremsier, " had it not been for whom," says Stitný,
" all these books which I have written would perhaps
never have existed."

Thomas of Stitný was born about the year 1325, as
is collected from his own writings, but nothing is known
about his parents, except that he was brought up and
educated by them, in all probability in their ancestral
tower of Stitný.   This was usual with the better class
of parents, there being at that time no schools but

those attached to monasteries. He speaks with especial
affection of his widowed grandmother, who resided
with the family. "I always remember," says he,
" how little regard, when I wanted to marry, I paid
to what I used to hear when young from my grandmother, who was a very excellent woman, of an honest
simplicity, and who used to say: 'Yea, dear Lord! how
is it that widows have a greater recompense than
married folk? yet how much better and quieter a life
do we have than in marriage!'" Such words, as Erben
remarks, are not to be heard except where single-hearted
love and true content are dominant in a family. It is
doubtful whether Stitný had any brothers, but he had
two sisters, Peltrata and Anna, respecting whom he
gives direction to his children in his last will. Of his
wife nothing is known but the deep affection with
which he speaks of her loving care for her children and
her early death. "Ye see and have seen how your mother
loved you for naught, without your having first done
any good to her. And if you will note it, I also love
you; were it not for you, I should have lived very dif-
ferently. . . . Wherefore always remember your mother,
how earnestly and lovingly she brought you up, with

more trouble than many mothers ; and entreat God
with earnest desire that He will be pleased to be
gracious to her and give Himself to her in recompense.
Even though she has by God's appointment departed
from the world, her remembrance and her love ought
not for that reason to depart from your hearts. And
if ye shall thus love us twain, considering that it is
impossible to recompense a father and mother to the
full, recompense us by loving each other more, for we
brought each one of you up just as affectionately as
another."

Stitný was about twenty-three years old when the
University of Prague was founded ; he appears to have
entered it at once and attached himself to the faculty
of arts, although he never took the degree of Master
of Arts. And he paid the greatest attention to the sermons of Conrad Waldhäuser and Milicz of Kremsier, as
appears from several passages of his writings, of which
I shall now only quote one, from chapter 200 of his
last work :—" And certain it is that this was so with
regard to the priest Conrad and the priest Milicz, who
were honourable, faithful, and steadfast preachers of
the word of God at Prague, the one to the Germans

and the other to the Bohemians; because they spoke against the fact that people were living in holy orders in an unholy manner, many thundered against them with arrogant and unjust words, and even now they are evil spoken of by those who say to evil, that it is not evil, and again of those good men, that they were evil." Stitný agreed with Milicz in recommending a frequent reception of the Holy Communion, or as he terms it, "the body of God," yet advises his children during their early youth to be contented with receiving it once a year, at Easter. He complains of Charles IV.'s excessive imposition of subsidies (*bernie*) for the purchase of the margravate of Brandenburg, which he appears to consider effected rather from dynastic motives than for the general good. Of the depreciation of the coinage he speaks very severely, concluding his denunciation with these words: "Ah! kings and lords! rule here in such wise, that ye condemn fraud and wrong, and do not commit them yourselves!" In one point he appears to have disagreed with Matthias of Janow, whose aversion to images was truly Protestant. "I am not one of those," says Stitný, "who have said that there ought not to be any images among

Christians; I think that they have proceeded too far; for we can have images instead of writing for a remembrance of such things, but not so as for an image to be any likeness of God."

In important and doubtful matters he gladly consulted celebrated men, and accepted instruction from them, and in particular submitted his first original work for revision and correction "to the master of extraordinary intelligence and wonderful memory, Albert, who was the first Bohemian who obtained the degree of Master in Holy Scripture in the University of Paris." Alluding to the disputes on the question of transubstantiation, raised by Wicliffe's books in the University of Prague, he says: "Ah! now am I in my seventieth year, yet have some masters moved me so that I cannot say for certain whether it is still bread in that Sacrament, under which is also the body of God, or whether it ceases to be bread, and is converted into the body of God. And this latter I have held, thinking that the Church had settled itself thereupon; and, according to this conception, I have set it down in some of my books, and other things appertaining thereto I have also set down; but these masters have shown me by sufficiently probable proof that it is still bread in the sacrament, and also the body of God. But I will rather say, 'I do not know what it is,' than say this or that, when even the Church has not yet settled itself thereon." But in his latest works, the manuscript of which was written in 1399, before the University of Prague had declared its views, he says: " Although a certain fear terrifies me, drawing me from this subject, nevertheless, hoping in God's help, I will not let it pass on account of my littleness. I will utter with my lips what my heart believes respecting this dear sacrament. If I should say aught unwisely, I declare that I intend to hold nothing but what is held by the Christian community and the University of Prague. And I entreat kindly correction from those of better understanding than myself, although from that, with regard to which I know how I ought to believe, I will not depart to follow anybody."

Very little is known of Stitný's life, except that between 1381 and 1394 he was compelled to have recourse to legal proceedings to recover his estate from a tenant who refused to pay the rent. Neither is the date of his death known with any certainty, but merely

K

that he was living at the age of seventy-four. I will
now proceed to give specimens of his style, manner,
and sentiments, and will commence with extracts from
the two prefaces to his first original work, " Of General
Christian Matters." The first preface begins thus :—

" My God hath commanded me, as he hath every
father, to lead you, my children, in his ways, and show
him to you. This is testified by the books of the old
law. It has therefore been the more agreeable to me
to write you these books, in order that what you now
perhaps, from your youth, cannot understand or remember of what I tell you, you may afterwards, when
perhaps I shall be dead, read therein, and understand
what it means ; and likewise that you may be able to
converse profitably together about that which appertains to salvation, or may be able to interest yourselves as well as those with whom you associate,
by reading in them, and that especially on festivals
at home in the village, where there is no sermon
or vespers. And likewise I counsel you to read
in them by yourselves, and particularly for this reason,
that you may question me when there is anything that
you do not understand as you read. For after my death

you will not, perhaps, so soon have anyone who will explain such a matter to you ; and it is very profitable to ask questions, when the person is suitable, with regard to what one does not understand as one reads. But it is not always suitable for damsels to inquire even of priests, unless on both sides they are very discreet, well-acquainted, and suitable. It is better sometimes to remain as one is, understanding that one does not understand, rather than ask questions of any and everybody.

" I have written you two sets of volumes, composing these first ones out of my own head, as seemed fitting, from what I have read anywhere, or heard in sermons or from learned men, or have been able to excogitate myself, that was adapted to the subject of which I was writing ; but the second set I found ready collected or composed by somebody else in Latin, and translated into Bohemian ; and I have written down there what they are. But these first ones I have divided into six sets of books :—

" The first are of faith and of hope and of love.

" The second of virgins, of widows, and of married people.

" The third, of the master of a family, of the mistress, and of the household.

" The fourth, how the nine orders of people bear the similitude of the nine choirs of angels.

" The fifth, how the devil tempts us.

" The sixth, how we purify ourselves from our sins. And, if I add a seventh or eighth, they will be here also.

" Whatever you find in these volumes, that hold, if you understand it, unless good people, and learned in the Scripture, prove to you that it is ill-written, so that it cannot in any wise be reconciled with Holy Scripture. For learned men, who are good, if they find anything that will bear a twofold meaning—a good and an evil one—turn it not to the evil, but to the good meaning."

Still more interesting is that part of the second preface, in which Stitný gives his reasons for writing in his native tongue, and defends the principles on which he does so :—

"I was instigated by a sermon of St. Augustine's to write Bohemian books, relating to Holy Scripture, with the greater boldness; for from it anyone can observe how good a thing it is to read Holy Scripture. And those who condemn Bohemian books, even if good ones, wishing, perhaps, to appear the only possessors of wisdom, may well dread the vengeance of God when they recollect how guilty those are who would wish to stop letters and needful messages therein, preventing the Lord God, the Everlasting Bridegroom, from instructing by them his Bride in his will, and comforting her in her distress. Yea, anyone would rightly be terrified who should stop a king's letters which he sends to his queen, if he learnt that the king knew it. And how much greater is the Lord God than any king! How much dearer to him is his Bride—that is, any soul that longeth after him—than was ever queen dear to any king ! Wiser men understand this, and know that a Bohemian is as precious to Him as a Latinist. If they like, they will do well to inquire of St. Paul as to this matter. . . . And note this also, dear brethren, that Holy Scripture is, as it were, letters sent us from our own fatherland. For our fatherland is Paradise, and our relatives are the patriarchs and prophets, the apostles and martyrs, and our fellow-citizens are the angels with whom we ought to be, and our king is

Christ. But when Adam sinned, then were we cast out
into the exile of this world. But because our king is
so merciful, more so than anyone can imagine, He
hath been pleased to send us by patriarchs and prophets the Holy Scripture—missionary letters, as it
were—whereby He invites us to return to our fatherland, and points out the way. And if this is so, dear
brethren, what mean those servants who are so ne-
glectful of their Lord, that they will not even read
the letters from Him, in which He invites them to His
blissful kingdom! . . . And if St. Augustine has thus
beautifully proved in that oration that it is good to
read Holy Scripture at home also, why need I urge
anybody any more to read these books? He will see
himself that they are scented with Holy Scripture,
and that they teach what is good, if he will read them.
And first they teach common things, but afterwards
he will find deeper things in them; and there will be
no one, whether old or young, but will be able to pass
time profitably with them, if only the word of God be
not offensive to him. But I entreat anyone who shall
read them, not to weigh the words overmuch, but to
seek the meaning; for I have sometimes said ' wood to

the vine-stock,' and peradventure he will find more thereof. And now I will begin in the name of God, and first from the foundation of Christian faith."

I will now proceed to the work itself, and shall select my first specimen from the first book, p. 35, and the section " How we ought to love God :"—

"No man can love God too much ; for however much He is loved—I do not say here in this world, but by all the saints in heaven—He is worthy of still greater love. Unless I thought fit to say that it is excessive love of God when a person injures himself from a good will by excessive suffering. But this He hath not commanded ; therefore this would not be from proper love, but from folly. This too is excessive love—or, I should better say, it is not love, but folly ; for no saint ever loved God with such love—when it is said : ' It is proper to love God in such a manner as not to desire any recompense from Him, that it may not be a hireling and slavish love.' I know that I ought not to love Him for any other recompense which is not Him-self, if I wish to love Him rightly. But if I love Him, then I would gladly possess Him ; and thus I cannot love Him without desiring to possess Him : and thus

I desire a recompense, viz. to possess Him.   And what
manner of love would that be, if anyone were to say
to me, 'I love you, but I pay no regard to you'?   And
if such love cannot be pleasing to a poor creature like
myself, how can it be pleasing to God, if a person were
to love Him without desiring to possess Him?''

In p. 77 advice is given to the young ladies of the
day, which would have come very well from the lips of
Huss.

"A second enemy of virgin purity, is wandering
about in foreign lands, from street to street and from
house to house, and even, to tell the truth, after indulgences.   In truth God is just as able to grant indulgences to one who, not from scorn, does not traverse the
world in search of them, but for some cause is in one
place and earnestly desires them, staying at home in
contrition and devotion, as the bishop or pope to one
who goes here or there.   It is the case sometimes
that a person gathering berries or plucking cherries,
when he has some already in his basket, espies others
on a branch difficult of access, or on a steep rock, and
wishing to reach them, soon scatters those which he
had before.   Even so is it often the case that, wishing to

obtain indulgences by pilgrimages, people sometimes
scatter what they already possessed. Much evil occurs
through this wandering, yea, it is written that Jacob's
daughter suffered rape through such wandering, and
much evil has happened through it. And what is
written is all written for our learning."

In p. 100 we find a passage extremely noble and
beautiful in itself, and also interesting as illustrating
the belief in and practice of witchcraft in Bohemia in
the fourteenth century :—

" A wise and noble mistress is like the moon. For
as the moon receives all its beauty from the sun, so
has she honour from her husband, if they look upon
each other faithfully and truly with true love, so that
there is no impediment between them through which
true love may vanish. As we see, when the earth is
between the sun and the moon, because the sun cannot look directly upon the moon owing to it, the moon
immediately vanishes ; if the sun also were to lose
its beauty, the moon would not be beauteous at all.
Therefore those mistresses do err who hold their husbands cheap or ridicule them, or who say to anyone
whatsoever, without very urgent need, what is to the

disgrace of their husbands. It is often the case that
many a wife thinks that her husband is only honoured
through her, and that he is in no respect advantageous
to her ; and she often thinks that she is thrown back
through him, because it seems to her that, if she had
him not, she would order her affairs much better ; then
it comes to pass, that when she is left by herself, then,
and not till then, does she know what trouble is, and
matters are much worse ordered than before ; and she
will have greater shame than if she had not spoken
against her husband before others. Therefore every
wise wife ought to love her husband and not to pride
herself above him on account of her birth or her wit ;
for a wife has honour through her husband more than
a husband through his wife. But as the light which
the moon has from the sun is little, since it has none
from itself, so likewise is the honour of this world but
little. For as the moon shines not in the day but only
in the night, and nevertheless makes night more cheerful, so will that honour be naught in that eternal day.
Therefore let us do what we do, not only for the present honour of praise here below, but while we avoid
not that honour for the sake of good example to

our neighbours, let us not wish to be satisfied with praise and honour here below, but tasting that it is pleasant and knowing a better, let us strive the more earnestly for that. And therefore a good mistress ought to avoid all faults before God and man, and do as much good as she can, and above all let her not defile the Christian faith in herself by any witchcraft; not as filthy women seek their husbands' love by the power of the devil, saying, 'A husband unbewitched is like peas without salt;' but a noble mistress of a family will draw her husband to her by good qualities and the gift of God."

In an " address to spiritual persons " (*pomluva k duchovním*) in the 4th book, p. 124, occurs a passage well worth extracting :—

" Neither can I pass over this in silence, for it often occurs among men that some one shines greatly with love to God, until he as it were burns just like a live coal, so that another might be kindled from him; but when a little adversity encounters him, he goes out, he turns black. And another will seem to be cold in the love of God, but when adversity encounters him, then and not till then does he exhibit heat; for love had been latent in him, but was greater than in the former. Just as limestone, if it burns, afterwards becomes cold, but if water is poured upon it becomes hot, and a hot, bright coal burns greatly with heat, but if you pour a little water upon it goes out.   Therefore I say this, let not the devout condemn all men, although there are some whom they do not see blazing with love, for God knows Himself who are His, and all is kept from us in uncertainty ; he who is blazing may go out in temptation, and in him who seems cold, love may increase in adversity.   Mark what God answered to Elias when he said, 'Ah ! Lord ! they have cast down thy altars, and slain thy prophets, and I alone am left, and they seek my life.' God answered him saying, ' Say not that thou art alone, I have reserved for myself 7,000 men who have not served devils.' "

Some remarks on the monks and friars of the day are worthy of extraction (p. 136):—

" And thus they have fallen away in love, they have not the peace of God in the mind, they do not rejoice with God in devotion, but quarrel, hate each other, condemn each other, priding themselves against each other, for love has sunk low in them on account of avarice, because they have forsaken God for money, breaking his holy laws and the oath of their own promise. And besides this (which is the most dreadful wickedness), they are irritated, they are annoyed at every good preacher or every good man who understands their error ; they would gladly make him out a heretic that they may have greater freedom for their cunning. And if they insinuate themselves to be the confessors of any conspicuous persons, they flatter those whom they know to be glad to listen to flattery, and if these are wise people, so that they dare not flatter them in evil, yet they pay no regard to bringing them from good to better, unless they give them gifts. Neither is this surprising : if they are unfaithful to their own souls, seeking cunning excuses against their rule, how can they be faithful to other souls ? "

In p. 142 Stitný returns to his favourite subject, Holy Scripture, and thus addresses students of theology :—

" It seems to me that this too is an important thing for the young who desire to gain instruction in Holy Scripture, to know that Holy Scripture is like a very wonderful river, so that the greatest elephant cannot ford it, but floats in it, yet a lamb can ford it—

that is to say, he who is proud does not allow the truth to move him, lest people should say, ' he has descended from his position.' Such a one is like an elephant that cannot bend his knees; and although he be of the highest intellect, he floats in Holy Scripture, and that especially if he claims to understand it all. But he who understands where he does not understand, that man by virtue of humility, like the lamb, can wade in Holy Scripture. Therefore the great elephants ought not to frighten or hinder the lambs from cooling themselves by wading in Holy Scripture, against the burning of worldly desires. If they are lambs they will not sink, they will say, ' We do not understand this.' If anything transcends their understanding, they will not be ashamed to confess it, and if they can be instructed by anyone, they will be glad to receive it; if they cannot, they will commit it to God, saying : ' If not here, yet there, O Lord, with thee, we shall understand this better.' "

In p. 166 the subject of private war is handled, and as this was quite an institution in the Middle Ages on the continent, I shall extract the passage for its historical value :—

" War is righteous on the side of one's lord, when
that lord wages a rightful war ; and even if the lord
be in the wrong, if it be not manifestly against the
Church, so that the Church does not excommunicate
him. And if his stewards or knights do not know
him to be in the wrong, they will not be wrong in
aiding him, but they would be wrong if they did not
aid him. And if thy lord appeareth in the wrong,
unless thou knowest for certain that he is in the wrong
in the dispute, thou mustest still consider rather that
he is in the right, for peradventure there is something
secret therein which thy lord is not bound to tell thee.
And therefore those who do not like to wage wrongful
wars ought to seek righteous and God-fearing lords
before war involves them, and avoid those with regard to whom it is impossible to hope that they will
be glad to abide by the right. As regards those wars
then which the landed proprietors (*vladykstvo*) have
together here in the country, I understand the matter
thus : Each may on a sudden repel sudden injury and
defend himself and his people against violence. But
so far as he has time for consideration, he ought first
of all to prove his rights by law ; and proving them by

law, then, and not till then, ought he, if he can, to extort them by force. Or he ought to complain of his injuries here in Bohemia to the king ; and if the king permits thee to make war, even without proving thy rights at law, if thou art in the right, thou mayest make war. But with one who is in the same legal position as thyself, thou mustest not wage war by thine own power with crafty intent; what good then would there be in the law or the king ?   And likewise it ought to be known, that he who wages war with another and is in the wrong, is bound to make good to him all the damages that he and his people have inflicted ; and also to his own people what they have lost therethrough. But he who wages war and is in the right, all that he conquers from his adversary is his according to law; and if his people suffer losses in his cause, he is not bound to make it good to them, for it is their duty to risk goods and life with their lord for his rights ; nevertheless, so far as he can, it would be proper to compensate them."

In p. 186 a brief passage in the fifth book " On the goad of the conscience " merits translation :—

" A man ought also to draw and lift the goad of the conscience, observing what is the good towards which he should direct his course. And the prophet Michah saith: 'I will show thee, O man, what is good and what the Lord requireth of thee : to do righteousness and love mercy, and to be diligent in walking with thy God.' Therefore it is important to think over these three things, that a man may direct himself towards righteousness, towards mercy, and towards earnestness in the ways of God. For a man thinks over a matter till he takes delight in it ; he takes delight in it till he will perform in act that in which he has taken delight. Thus, that he may direct his course toward righteousness, it is proper to reflect upon it in the mind ; for neither the morning star nor the evening star is so marvellous in its brightness as is righteousness. And we must diligently observe this, if we wish to be righteous, not to remain indebted to any one, but give to each what appertains to him : honour to whom honour, tribute to whom tribute, custom to whom custom ; and so also in other things, as St. Paul enjoins. But whether we be indebted to our inferiors, our equals, or our superiors, it is not right to remain indebted to anyone, withholding the debt. And this we can observe for ourselves : to do to others the same that we should wish from our inferiors, our equals, or our superiors."

I will take leave of the fifth book with the following extract : —

" The second path which leads a man to God is enlightenment. And the better a man can know the truth from being enlightened in understanding, the more like will he be to the angels of the second choir of the highest hierarchy. Therefore he who desires to be enlightened must betake himself to the ray of understanding, and when this ray comes from the true sun, it is straight, bright, and hot : straight, not going circuitously ; bright, dispelling darkness ; and hot, warming the man who has his conversation in it with the love of God. For there is also another ray, but not straight, nor hot with the heat that gives life, nor so bright : that is the wisdom of this world. How that wisdom goes circuitously and not straight, is to be seen in that the wise of this world amass much that they may be valued, and desire to be valued that they may amass much ; aim at pleasure in order that through gratifying themselves they may live longer, and wish to live that they may have pleasure. How it is not hot with the heat that giveth light, is to be seen in that people are by that ray not kindled but chilled in the love of God. And how it is dark, mark thyself, in that ofttimes a man obstinately aims at that which is evil to him, even according to the world. Therefore I say, let him who desires to be enlightened betake himself to the ray of understanding, not that of worldly wisdom, but that which leads straight, shines brightly, and kindles to the love of God, that is to true wisdom, that thou mayest be grateful for that which thou recognizest as coming from the good God, and desire to advance further therefrom and come to God."

I will now bring to an end my specimens of Stitný's first original work with two brief extracts from, and part of, the conclusion of the sixth book. The first is from the section on Wedlock :—

"Even as iron, though black itself, yet when thoroughly heated by fire, while remaining the same, hath not its own beauty, but all that of fire, so we, though we are anything but beautiful, shall yet shine for ever and ever with the brilliancy of our eternal husband, and be honoured with his honour, as a wife hath honour through the honour of her husband."

The second alludes to the notion of a person in mortal sin ceasing temporarily or permanently to be a member of the Church, which played so prominent a part in the trial of Huss, and which has generally, though wrongly, been supposed to have originated with Wicliffe :—

" And so long as anyone pays no regard to God, will not perform his commandments, will not leave all that God hath forbidden, what else is he but an enemy of God ? He is not a member of the Church, he has fallen out of the unity of the Church, and outside of the Church there is no remission of sins."

The whole work concludes as follows (p. 286) :—

" With this let my first set of books be ended, which I composed and arranged as I thought good, firstly, for you, my children, and next for everyone to whom they may be comforting and whom they may assist in the understanding of divers things profitable for Christians to understand. And because I am a man, I may have erred, and I am not even a magister, although I spent the first years of my youth in the University, and have lived in the world, and still endure it; nevertheless I delight in occupying myself with books as much as I can. And I have not written these books with the intent that every word in them should be weighed, like the language of those books which appertain to the Bible, but let him to whom the general meaning appears right hold it fast until he be taught better by those who have a right to teach. But it is a marvellous thing in some people, that they will not mark whether what is said is the truth, but only want to know who says it. But did not even a she-ass by the Holy Spirit speak truth to Balaam ? Does not pure water sometimes flow in decayed conduits ? Therefore what truth there is here is from God, and if any error is committed it is through myself, and I beg that if I have strayed from the road it may be kindly corrected, and also if a fault has been committed while going along the road ; for one man goes along the road keeping more to the right hand, another to the left, and a third goes along the middle of the road, and there are some who, as they go, will keep first to one side and then to the other : therefore if I have but been somewhere on the road, I pray you kindly pardon me.

"Again, if I have written anything here which I did not find in Scripture, I desire to be repaid, when that Samaritan comes who gave two pence to him to whom he commended the wounded man, and said: 'What thou spendest on him more, I will repay.' And as to my having written something in this set of books beyond what I promised in the beginning, I excuse it by having said, 'If then I add a seventh or eighth book, this will also be here.' What more there is here, return to me, Lord, as well as to those who shall read in them or hear them, on the Sabbath of the seventh and eighth days!"

I come now to Stitný's last corrected and rewritten edition of this work, which was printed by the Matice Czeská in 1873. In many instances the wording is identical, in others great alterations have been made. But translations and original writings are so blended together into one whole in this latter work, that it is sometimes very difficult to be sure whether a striking passage is original or translated. Either work, however, may safely challenge a comparison with anything extant and originally written in the English language, till we come to the great work of Hooker himself. An address to the learned in pp. 78 and 79 is very striking :—

"The second choir in the highest hierarchy is named cherubin, that is, fulness of knowledge or science; and they may be so called because, perhaps, they have love to God from having that fulness of knowledge and understanding. As perhaps the members of the first choir have their understanding or other divine gifts from their fervent love of God, as we see that many have great and right understanding from their great love to God, and, without having learned much, nevertheless are in unison with Holy Scripture, while others first began to love God after reading the Scripture and learning; and thus I have compared the first class to the seraphin and the second to the cherubin. For it is especially through devout lovers of God that God hath given us understanding in Holy Scripture. But this, moreover, I say to you, the devout, and you who wish to be spiritual and who claim to understand everything. Do not contemn Holy Scripture : look whether your ideas be in unison with it, and if then you have no need of Scripture, at any rate it is for inferior people. All that is written by divine inspiration is profitable for instruction in right understanding. And even St. Paul, though he had received instruction in

the school of heaven, and was certain that he had a
right understanding, nevertheless went to the other
apostles who had here on earth received instruction
from Christ, and conferred with them about what he
taught people.   Therefore, I always say : The greater
one is, and the higher he strives to soar, the more cir-
cumspect let him be ! for the devils that fell from the
higher choirs are much more crafty than those that fell
from the lower ones.   And these peradventure especially seek to undermine, deceive, and seduce those who
bear greater resemblance to the higher choirs.   Thus
the learned ought very diligently to beware of these
crafty devils, who craftily draw learned and intelligent
people to convert their learning, intelligence, and knowledge into cunning and craft, and to enter into pride and
arrogance and into envy of others, wishing to be themselves the only people who appear learned. And hence
it is the case, even as a certain brother, Tohodoben, has
put in one of his tracts intituled, '*Horologium Sapien-
cie*' (the 'Clock of Wisdom'), that he saw in a vision
in a school a number of magisters, and a silver sword
among them, and each wanted to have the sword, but
took much more pains to strike it out of another's hand

than to get hold of it himself. This similitude rebukes the learned for envy, as each of those envious learned men wanted to obtain the glory of being learned and scientific himself. And that glory is signified by the silver sword, which each wanted, but was more eager to deprive another of that glory, by condemning in some respect his wise statements or books, striking as it were the sword out of his hand, than to do anything of the kind himself. Therefore it is that magisters are not willing to write such books, not wishing them to be condemned in any respect by others. But Christ said, 'If these shall hold their peace, the stones will cry out.' And thus Bridget, an old woman, and Milicz, who was not a magister, have written books; neither has the writer of these books desired the name of a learned man."

Stitný's matured ideas on the subject of secular pastimes will not be uninteresting (p. 93):—

" I will say first, that gentlemen may sometimes take recreation with moderation in pastimes, but not till the claims of what is important have been satisfied. But as to their taking for a pastime what is downright pride and injurious in property and life, such pastimes

I cannot commend. I speak thus with regard to the tourney, because that injurious pastime ought not to be termed a pastime, and the tourney is prohibited in the spiritual laws. Thus it has been appointed as a penalty for those who have not observed the Church ordinance therein, that he who is killed in a tournament, or dies from an injury there received, is not to be buried in consecrated ground, not even if he has confessed and received the holy oil. Dances, too, have much evil attaching to them—pride, licentiousness, envy. Therefore, although dancing is not in itself an evil thing for secular people, yet holy men condemn dances as being the cause of much evil. Games at dice, too, are an ill pastime, for avarice will ere long be there.

"Of hunting I say this, that those hunts which are connected with vainglory—as, for instance, awaiting the attack of the bear or boar—are not good. It is not good to risk life without other necessity for that vainglorious idea. And briefly I say, in every pastime let each man look to it himself, that his pastime do not pass the bounds of moderation or of the Church ordinance, and that he do not devote himself to the pastime. We are not placed here to give ourselves up to pastimes, but to do what is needful for ourselves or our neighbours, each according to his station ; and if we do this, people may properly, at the proper time, according to their station, take recreation in pastimes."

I will conclude my extracts by giving what appear to be Stitný's own views on the actual reception of the Eucharist :—

"This, too, I say with regard to this sacrament: its importance does not reside in its being gazed at and in doing obeisance to it,[1] but it ought to be taken and received as nourishment. But there are three things to observe in connection with this sacrament.

"One is the visible sacrament itself, which, by its visible similitude, signifieth an invisible spiritual grace; that is, as visible corporeal food strengthens the bodily life, so does the invisible power of this sacrament strengthen the spiritual life.

"The second thing to be noticed in this sacrament is what is in it; for here is the very glorified body of the Son of God as it is in its glory, with both its soul and its deity.

[1] How like this is to the sentiment of our 28th Article!

" The third thing to be understood is this: that this sacrament signifies something that is not in it; for it signifies the whole body of the holy Church—that is, the whole Christian community—but that is not there, but Christ himself is there, who is the head of all the holy Church. And it is by this similarity that this sacrament signifies all the holy Church, in that as one loaf is made up of many grains, so is the whole Church one body made up of many people, the head whereof is Christ. I have for this reason touched upon this, that it may be understood that some people receive the sacrament itself, but not that which is in it nor that which it signifies, and they, receiving the sacrament thus, receive to themselves condemnation.

" Others sometimes do not receive the sacrament, but receive that which is in the sacrament, and that which the sacrament signifies; that is, they receive Christ, and enter into the unity of the holy Church, so that they will be one body with the devout.

" A third class receive both the sacrament and that which is in it and that which it signifies.

" I say, too, whoso doth not receive the true faith of Christ, and whoso is not by grace in the unity of the holy Church, so that he retains anger or hatred against anyone who is a member of the holy Church, or if by any disorder whatever of mortal sin he is not in the unity of the holy Church, such a one ought not to approach the sacrament, for he would approach it fraudulently, pretending that which he hath not. Such a one, if he received the sacrament, would receive condemnation."

Only three of Stitný's sermons are given by Erben in the " Výbor," from two of which I give specimens. In the course of the sermon on the Circumcision, which is addressed to haughty lords, he says with reference to the fashion of rivalry in splendour, &c. :—

" But there will be no excuse before God for allowing oneself to be overpowered by a vain idea, for God hath given man reason in order that he may oppose vain things and seek eternal and abiding honour, seeing by reason, that the honour of worldly glory is like that rotten wood which shines only in the night, but the day shows it to be a rotten thing. Likewise, this world is night in comparison with that eternal day. Here worldly glory seems light, but when it comes to the brightness of that eternal day, it will be

manifest that all the praise of this world is a decayed
thing, and a proud or licentious man in such magnifi-
cence is very rottenness."

And in one of his sermons for Palm Sunday he
says :—

" Humility is the preservation of the other virtues ;
for even if a man has amassed other virtues, without
humility he will lose them all.   Just as if he had piled
up a heap of dust and a wind should come and dis-
perse it all ; even so haughty pride, if it comes into
the heart, will destroy all good.   Let a man have
science, let him have wisdom, let him have beauty,
it will spoil it all, if therewith be pride.   And therefore humility is a necessary virtue, the office of which
is to expel pride, to preserve the other virtues, and to
keep us in the truth.   But let us mark what humility
is.   Humility is a voluntary lowering of the mind from
observation of one's own frailty and other deficiencies.
And St. Bernard saith : Humility is the virtue whereby
a man, rightly knowing himself, becomes vile in his
own eyes.   We ought to have a twofold knowledge of
self, and each will exhort unto humility, when we come
rightly to know what we are and what we are not.

Through each of these we have cause for humility, observing that by ourselves we are infirmity; nay, even if we are something, we have received it by God's gift, through his grace. How, and of what can we be proud? St. Paul saith: What hast thou that thou didst not receive, that is, by gift from God? And if thou didst receive it, why dost thou boast, as if thou didst not receive, but hadst it of thyself? Lo! from recognition of this the greatest man, of whatsoever worldly, bodily, or spiritual gifts of God he be possessed, may be humble, but not proud; for he has nothing of himself, nor can he have anything longer than God permits. This humility is a quality of the good and wise, who enter not into refractoriness or pride on account of what God has given them beyond others, not seeking reputation thereby with vainglorious mind; but the more of God's gifts they have, the more humble will they be, giving God the glory."

I pass now to Stitný as a philosopher with tendencies rather Realistic than Nominalistic, but never losing sight of practical theology, and always endeavouring to reconcile revelation with science—that is of course with the science of his day, which rested on the basis of the Ptolemaic system.

In chapter iii. of the " Rozmluvy Nábozné " the children say : " We wish to ask something about God, that we may obtain your statements—for the more we hear about Him, the clearer does our understanding become, and contemplations so wondrous excite greater love—as to whether it is ever possible to know that, and delight oneself everlastingly in that, which thus excels all things by its glory. Therefore tell us, if all is in God, where God is, or where He was before He created the world ? "

The father replies: "I told you, if you will remember, everything is in God, not as in a place, or as in a purse, or as in a house ; but everything is in His power and in His wisdom and in His love. But if you say, Where is He ? you say habitually, 'Who art in heaven.' And the prophet saith : If I go up into heaven, thou art there ; if I go down into hell, thou art there also. Let me say briefly : God is everywhere, but in one way in one place, in another in another. As the soul is everywhere in the human body, but by more excellent operation in the head, so is He in heaven by more excellent operation than elsewhere. But He is not in heaven nor in any place whatever in such manner that the place so contains Him as to be occupied by Him. There is no place but that He is there in His being, which the Latinists term essence, and likewise there is no place that contains Him. And thus God is and dwells in light, which it is impossible to approach ; I do not mean the brightness of corporeal light to the eyes, but I speak of the inward eyes. And thus I say : God in Himself is incomprehensible. But you have now heard no little concerning Him, if you know that He is not in any place so that it contains Him, neither is there any place where He is not. And by a certain excellent operation, as all is in Him, so is He in all ; and as He existed before He created the world by Himself in His own glory, there He is still. For He did not create the world, that He might have a place to be in ; nor is He so in the world, that He would fall if the world were to perish. And therefore God is that, than which nothing greater can be conceived."

In chapter ix. the children inquire how we are to observe God's wisdom in His creation, and in part of his reply the father says : " This world is as it were a

M

kind of books common to all, which are written by the
hand of God, that is by the power and wisdom of God,
and every creature in particular is a word in these
books, which are for the display of His power and wisdom.   And as it is the case that an illiterate person,
looking at books, sees words written, but understands
not what they signify ; even so an unwise man, who
only proceeds after the manner of a stupid beast and
does not apply his mind to God, looks into the form at
present existing in the visible creation, but does not
understand what and why it is ; but a spiritual man,
who can judge everything, sees inwardly in that beauty
which is visible in the creation, how wondrous and
great is the wisdom of God, which has thus beautifully
arranged it all.   Therefore the works of God are wonderful to all : the unwise admire only the external
beauty and fairness of the beauteous creation, and incline thereto with love ; but whoso is wise apprehends
more deeply the wisdom of God through that which he
sees externally ; as in these my books one man praises
the fact that they are handsome and well got up ; another, that there is good handwriting in them ; while
a third commends the internal meaning which is in the

handwriting. Therefore it is good to admire the fact that God has arranged so many things so beautifully and appropriately; but it is also good for him who understands how to turn the internal beauty of God to spiritual advantage, not to incline with love to the beautiful and appropriately arranged creation, but turn with love from the creation to the Creator, who has carried it out with such regularity."

In the course of the work Stitný deals with the questions of "form," "quality" and "beauty"—that Cinderella, as Professor Hanus calls it, of the gifts of God during the Middle Ages—in a manner most interesting to a Bohemian, who looks with delight upon the way in which he copes with the difficulties of his native tongue and makes it a proper exponent of philosophical terms and notions. But such discussions and such endeavours, however successful, would lose their entire effectiveness and interest in a foreign language, and I therefore now conclude my specimens of Stitný's philosophical writings.

And now I hope I may safely ask whether I have not exhibited enough from the rags and fragments left by the fires of Jesuits and the fangs of minor destroyers,

to prove that there was a high state of literary cultiva-
tion in Bohemia in the fourteenth century, which ren-
dered it a fit birthplace of such a movement as that
commonly known as the Hussite movement—a movement which kept the eyes of the civilized world upon
it for many years, which defied and resisted both Papacy
and Empire, and only perished because its nationality
was different from that of the great nation which inaugurated and carried out that other great movement
which is known as the Protestant Reformation. To
be of Slavonic, more especially of Czech nationality,
is enough in the eyes of many to call down a storm
of contempt, slander, and insinuation upon the devoted
head ; what wonder then if the oppressed and despised
Slavonians turn with hope towards that empire of Russia
which is simply too vast to be despised, and whose very
vastness almost renders the utmost efforts of slander
and insinuation impotent ?

Twice has a little Slavonic nation, the nation of the
Czechs, the inhabitants of Bohemia, performed services
of the highest order to the best interests of mankind ;
but never has it received the slightest recognition of
its services, abandoned as it was at the conclusion of the

Thirty Years War by its so-called allies to the tender mercies of its deadliest foes. Bohemia was the first country that succeeded in checking the wave of Tatar invasion which in the thirteenth century threatened to submerge the whole of Europe; it was Bohemia that opposed the first successful resistance to the arrogant claims and usurpations of the papacy, and that struggled successfully for liberty of conscience. To use the words of one of her own poets, Boleslaw Jablonský :—

> Bohemia 'twas, amongst the neighb'ring lands
>> That lighted erst the torch of wisdom free ;
> Bohemia's sons it was, whose valiant hands
>> Won for all Europe priceless liberty.

And again the same poet describes his heroic ancestors, with equal point and truth, as

> Bees. that their weapons knew with courage brave,
>> Right well to use in many a conflict rude,
> Bees, that their honey oft to others gave,
>> Yet earn'd but insult and ingratitude.

CHISWICK PRESS :—C. WHITTINGHAM, TOOKS COURT, CHANCERY LANE.

LIFE, LEGEND, AND CANONIZATION OF ST. JOHN NEPOMUCEN, Patron Saint and Protector of the Order of the Jesuits. London: Bell and Sons, 1873. 3s. 6d.

"Mr. Wratislaw has done good service in putting together the evidence and tracing the genesis of the myth in a compendious form."—*Saturday Review.*

NOTES AND DISSERTATIONS, principally on Difficulties of the Scriptures of the New Covenant. London: Bell and Sons, 1863. 7s. 6d.

"Mr. Wratislaw's Dissertations often claim, not without justice, the rank of new and independent contributions towards the correct appreciation of the subjects of which they treat. They deal, too, with texts or topics which have been from ancient times themes of controversy among expositors and theologians. He exhibits throughout high attainments and abilities as a scholar, and much independence and honesty as a theologian."—*Guardian.*

"Mr. Wratislaw is a very straightforward critic, who does not consider the duty of the illustrator of the New Testament writings to be adequately performed by repeating a mass of opinions and leaving difficulties just as they were before."—*Westminster Review.*

CPSIA information can be obtained at www.ICGtesting.com
Printed in the USA
BVOW06s0447110615

404047BV00005BA/9/P